MW01244893

GLOBAL CONNECTIONS

THE CHANGING GLOBAL ECONOMY

GLOBAL C🌐NNECTI🌐NS

America's Role in a Changing World
Changing Climates
The Changing Global Economy
Environment and Natural Resources
Feeding a Hungry World
The Human Population
Human Rights
One World or Many?
Pandemics and Global Health
Terrorism and Security

GLOBAL CONNECTIONS

THE CHANGING GLOBAL ECONOMY

ZORAN PAVLOVIĆ
SERIES EDITOR: CHARLES F. GRITZNER

CHELSEA HOUSE
PUBLISHERS
An imprint of Infobase Publishing

The Changing Global Economy
Copyright © 2010 by Infobase Publishing

All rights reserved. No part of this book may be reproduced or utilized in any form or by any means, electronic or mechanical, including photocopying, recording, or by any information storage or retrieval systems, without permission in writing from the publisher. For information contact:

Chelsea House
An imprint of Infobase Publishing
132 West 31st Street
New York, NY 10001

Library of Congress Cataloging-in-Publication Data
Pavlovic, Zoran.
  The changing global economy / by Zoran Pavlovic.
      p. cm. — (Global connections)
  Includes bibliographical references and index.
  ISBN 978-1-60413-283-0 (hardcover)
  1. Globalization—Economic aspects—Juvenile literature. I. Title.
II. Series.

  HF1359.P385 2009
  337—dc22   2009006648

Chelsea House books are available at special discounts when purchased in bulk quantities for businesses, associations, institutions, or sales promotions. Please call our Special Sales Department in New York at (212) 967-8800 or (800) 322-8755.

You can find Chelsea House on the World Wide Web
at http://www.chelseahouse.com

Text design by Annie O'Donnell
Cover design by Takeshi Takahashi

Printed in the United States of America

Bang EJB 10 9 8 7 6 5 4 3 2 1

This book is printed on acid-free paper.

All links and Web addresses were checked and verified to be correct at the time of publication. Because of the dynamic nature of the Web, some addresses and links may have changed since publication and may no longer be valid.

CONTENTS

INTRODUCTION

A GLOBAL COMMUNITY

Globalization is the process of coming together as a closely connected global community. It began thousands of years ago, when tribal groups and small hunting parties wandered from place to place. The process accelerated following Columbus's epic voyage more than five centuries ago. Europeans—an estimated 50 million of them—spread out to occupy lands throughout the world. This migration transformed the distribution of the world's peoples and their cultures forever. In the United States and Canada, for example, most people speak a West European language. Most practice a religious faith with roots in the ancient Middle East and eat foods originating in Asia.

Today, we are citizens of a closely interwoven global community. Events occurring half a world away can be watched and experienced, often as they happen, in our own homes. People, materials, and even diseases can be transported from continent to continent in a single day, thanks to jet planes. Electronic communications make possible the instantaneous exchange of information by phone, e-mail, or other means with friends or business associates almost anywhere in the world. Trade and commerce, perhaps more so than any other aspect of our daily lives, amply illustrate the importance of global linkages. How many things in your home (including your clothing) are of international origin? What foods and beverages have you consumed today that came from other lands? Could Northern America's economy survive without foreign oil, iron ore, copper, or other vital resources?

The GLOBAL CONNECTIONS series is designed to help you realize how closely people and places are tied to one another within the expanding global community. Each book introduces you to political, economic, environmental, social, medical, and other timely issues, problems, and prospects. The authors and editors hope you enjoy and learn from these books. May they hand you a passport to intellectual travels throughout our fascinating, complex, and increasingly "intradependent" world!

—*Charles F. Gritzner*
Series Editor

A CHANGING GLOBAL ECONOMY

On a sunny afternoon in many American communities, the farmer's market attracts people in search of fresh produce. Locally grown organic vegetables are popular among the health-savvy. Urban farmer's markets, for the most part, at least, attract produce sellers who do organic gardening as a hobby. They do it for enjoyment, rather than as a necessity for their basic economic survival. In the United States and Canada, food is very inexpensive. We may drive 10 or 20 miles (16–32 kilometers) just to shop in our favorite grocery store. Our dinners can even be purchased on the Internet and delivered by special trucks. We live in a wealthy postindustrial society in which people pay to have services performed. Few people in Northern America (the United States and Canada) have to worry about starving to death. Our nations' economic strength reflects our individual well-being.

Now imagine a community market someplace in Africa, south of the Sahara. There, small-scale gardening and animal herding are not done for fun. Crops are grown and livestock are raised to make ends meet. This is how many people survive. There are no spotless tomatoes or varieties of lettuce—from regular to officially certified as being organic—displayed on stands. Many residents, if lucky, earn a dollar per day, often even less. They may walk many miles to deliver basic products to be sold, such as grain, vegetables, eggs, or perhaps some milk. Their small profit will be used to purchase necessities for their children. At the end of the day, these farmers travel on foot many miles back to their village. The same process may be repeated the following day, and day after day. Local governments have no resources with which to provide appropriate financial help. They can do little to improve the economy. If drought, a locust plague, or storm damage strikes, widespread famine may occur.

GLOBAL ECONOMIC TRANSFORMATION

Until a century or two ago, most people practiced an economic lifestyle similar to that described in our African example. This way of life, often a day-to-day struggle for survival, changed little over thousands of years. Initially, it was based upon hunting, gathering, and perhaps fishing. Nearly everyone lived off the land. Later, in some locations, life began to revolve around primitive agriculture. A few people here and there began to grow their own crops and raise livestock. Except for the tiny ruling class and clergy, the vast majority of people cultivated fields or engaged in craft-based businesses.

With the dawn of agriculture about 10,000 to 12,000 years ago in some regions of the world, things began to change. As noted above, some people began to produce their own food, rather than obtain it through hunting, fishing, and gathering. Social scientists call this gradual event the Agricultural Revolution. And some believe that it brought about the most significant cultural change in human history. (*Culture*, as used in this book, refers to a people's way of life; it includes what they know, possess, and are able to do.) No longer were we wandering hunters and gatherers. Rather, we became food producers, overseeing fields of wheat, barley, rice, maize (corn), and other grains. With a food surplus, we could cluster together in larger numbers and live in one place. Soon, great civilizations arose from agricultural settlements along rivers such as the Tigris and Euphrates, Nile, Indus, and others.

In medieval times, European serfs (poor farm workers) cultivated the land to feed their own families. They also had to pay tribute to feudal landowners. Then, toward the end of the eighteenth century, something major occurred that drastically changed the direction of our civilization. It began in the British Isles. This radical change is known as the Industrial Revolution. In the early nineteenth century, the steam engine and railways indeed revolutionized the world. Transportation vastly improved, manufacturing blossomed, and the human population exploded. Later in the same century, electricity and petroleum began to provide energy. These developments further improved transportation, along with having many other uses.

Rapid urbanization (the growth of cities) went hand in hand with industrial development. Tall chimneys belching foul black smoke represented a sign of social and economic progress. The Industrial Revolution brought about a huge improvement in the general quality of life. More people went to school and became educated. Diet improved, as did medical care, resulting in a lengthening of human life expectancy. With jobs, people began to earn wages and become specialized in a specific trade. No longer were they self-sufficient "jacks of all trades, while masters of none."

Imagine, it has been just over two centuries since the British engineer James Watt improved the steam engine. And now we are sending spaceships to Jupiter and sampling the soil of Mars. During the past two centuries, life expectancy has more than doubled. Individual freedoms have improved significantly throughout much of the world. What previously appeared as unimaginable, such as an 80-year life span, is now an ordinary aspect of life. Northern American industrial development, in particular, was unmatched during this period. It was one of several factors that elevated the region to the status of a primary global economic power.

UNEQUAL DEVELOPMENT

The process of industrialization affected everyone differently. It takes time for major discoveries and innovations (formerly called "inventions") to be accepted and then spread elsewhere. Various factors influence uneven development. The kind of government a country has greatly influences its ability to progress economically. For example, some countries reject the free market capitalist system. This is especially true for countries with dictatorial governments that fear the loss of political control. Yet capitalism and democracy have been the driving forces of industrialization, economic growth, and prosperity for most countries. When nations fully embrace a free market system, they almost always experience an economic boom. They also undergo many positive social changes. Among those changes is people's desire to be in control of their own affairs and to seek individual freedoms.

Regimes like those in Communist North Korea or in Saudi Arabia, where the ruling family governs by a strict interpretation of Islamic law, severely limit personal liberties. North Korea lags far behind the rest of the world because of ideological repression. The Communists do not allow anything but government-controlled enterprise. In Saudi Arabia, kings of the House of Saud oversee economic development. They do so, however, in close cooperation with religious leaders who do not allow citizens to stray from rigid Islamic teachings. If not for vast oil production and reserves, Saudi Arabia would have remained the poorly developed country it was before oil was discovered.

Wars, as well, influence economic development, but mostly in negative ways. Civil wars bring destruction of a nation's economic base. This makes a country fall behind in an already highly competitive world. The former country of Yugoslavia is an example of such a nation. Before 1990, it was a moderately developed European country. In the decades following World War II, it managed to improve its agricultural economy. It also became more economically diverse by promoting industrial development. Although ruled by the Communist Party, the former Yugoslavia was more economically liberal than the Soviet Union and its Eastern European satellites. At the same time, however, many social and ethnic issues remained unresolved and severely suppressed. These issues exploded like a powder keg once the Communists lost their grip on power. Ethnic struggles erupted into a civil war that devastated local economies. Almost two decades later, some of them still struggle economically at a level close to that of the prewar era.

COMPETITIVE WORLD

The world, it is often said, is not a fair place. We support each other only when we have enough to share. Wealthy countries provide economic assistance to developing nations only because they have an abundance of food or other supplies. When circumstances worsen with global economic downturns, which happen periodically, international aid declines sharply. After all, everyone has to think of his or her own people first, even if others are affected by famine. The result is that some people and countries have more and others have less.

In the competitive global economic environment, wealth is not evenly distributed. Western Europe, Northern America, and several Asian nations hold the most wealth. Compared to the wealthy nations, less developed countries (LDCs) continue to significantly lag behind in economic development. Some people believe that this gap in well-being is immoral. They call for economic and political measures that would create a better global balance of wealth. Some even suggest that the gap between rich and poor nations is an example of economic imperialism. They

Western corporations learned that they could increase profits considerably by moving their manufacturing plants and other operations to less developed nations, where labor is cheap. This practice has impacted the entire global economy.

argue that the rich take advantage of the poor in order to make profits, while the poor receive few benefits, if any.

For example, a corporation from Europe may open a manufacturing plant in an Asian country where wages are low. There, workers assemble products that are shipped to markets in the United States and Canada. Labor costs are much lower than those the corporation would have to pay European workers. The difference represents a considerable savings, hence, a substantial profit to the company. Critics, however, argue that the Asian laborers should receive higher wages and a much larger portion of the corporation's income. Thus, they claim, the wealthy nations are becoming wealthier at the expense of poor countries. And the gap between rich and poor in the world is continuously widening.

Alternative views, however, remind us that we need to look at global economic connections from different perspectives. In the current system, even the poorer nations are wealthier today than ever before in their history. The main reason they are better off is a global economic system of expanding production and demand. In times long past, economies were strictly local. Today, they are increasingly global. Low wages and ample amounts of labor are the factors that made the poorer nations competitive in the first place.

The creation of economic wealth is a gradual process that largely depends upon the system of production and demand. If prices of products are too high for the American consumer because the European corporation has to pay Asian laborers higher wages, the profit will decline. Were this to occur, the corporation might decide to relocate. It would withdraw its investments in Asia and transfer them to some other part of the world, perhaps a country in Africa. Eager to attract foreign investments, African nations might offer a labor force willing to work for much lower wages. The result of this business shift might well be massive layoffs in the Asian country. In a competitive world, everyone is trying to make a profit. But making a "fast buck" is much more difficult than gradual step-by-step economic growth and development.

GLOBAL ECONOMIC CONNECTIONS

The year 2008 will be remembered as one of the most difficult times in American economic history. In a matter of a few months, the world's largest economy experienced a meltdown unparalleled in recent history. Real-estate prices plummeted and the stock market lost a quarter of its value in a period of several weeks. Projected losses surpassed trillion-dollar levels almost as if these astronomical amounts were just pocket change. The

WHERE IS IT FROM?

Harley-Davidson motorcycles, just like apple pie, are an American icon. In the early 1900s, two friends started a business in their Milwaukee, Wisconsin, garage. Their main supplier was a guy down the street. No one expected William S. Harley and Arthur Davidson to generate much attention with their products. Yet they did! By the 1920s, their company had become the world's largest motorcycle manufacturer. What helped this rapid development was America's involvement in two world wars. During the wars, Harley-Davidson was the main supplier of motorcycles to the U.S. military. Later on (and with generous help from the Hollywood motion picture industry), the company's motorcycles achieved cult status and became a revered symbol of American popular culture.

To assemble this truly American icon today, machinery and parts for the Milwaukee Harley-Davidson factory arrive from Europe, Japan, Latin America, and elsewhere. The interaction with many international businesses is required in order to produce a modern Harley-Davidson motorcycle. Buying parts from many specialized suppliers helps lower production costs and increases quality. So, as you have seen, something that is as "American" as apple pie is really the product of a global economic effort. (By the way, the apples, the wheat from which pie crust is made, and the sugar that sweetens the pie are all Asian in origin!)

most fascinating effect of the credit crisis was how rapidly it affected the rest of the world. In order to salvage their financial sectors and protect their citizens' investments, many governments abruptly took control over previously private banks. Others pumped money into financial markets just to have their economies stay afloat.

The 2008 economic crisis illustrates just how closely the global economy is connected. We have reached a moment in time when no country can survive an economic downturn on its own.

Globalization contributes to a condition of "guilt by association." When times are good, everyone profits. When the world's largest economy experiences serious problems, everyone suffers.

For example, the credit and housing crisis in the United States forces American consumers to spend less on electronics manufactured by a Japanese company in China. Thus, profits decline in both Japan and China. To compensate for losses, the Japanese and Chinese limit their investments in Africa. There, a number of nations count on foreign credit for their own development. With little money available for credit, the governments have to rely on printing more notes. This leads to inflation, which places the cost of many consumer products far beyond the financial reach of most people. Salaries for ordinary workers rarely follow a rise in the cost of consumer goods. Therefore, the ability of consumers to purchase products becomes even more difficult. With few buyers, shop owners begin to feel the pinch. In this way, it doesn't take long for the global economic system to become overloaded with financial troubles.

The consequences of unsound economic policies are harsh. We no longer live in a time when isolated nations can remain untouched by a damaging economic cycle. Today, everyone pays a price in some way during an economic downturn. Yet, for a country to isolate itself from global markets and insist on self-sufficiency is a recipe for even worse disaster. This is why most countries willingly participate in joint programs fostering economic cooperation. Global economic connections are here to stay. The purpose of this book is to analyze their relationships and to illustrate patterns and distributions of changing economic processes.

IS THE WORLD REALLY "FLAT"?

A look at an economic map of the world shows a great deal of diversity. People engage in many different economic activities. Often, these differences depend at least in part upon where they live. In coastal areas, for example, fishing may edge ahead of mining or agriculture as the primary economic activity. Most of the world's major shipping ports face oceans rather than internal water bodies. Agriculture takes advantage of natural elements such as location, soils, and climate. Mining occurs in areas rich in minerals. A people's economy is one of the most important indicators of their culture, or way of life. It reveals what they do now and also provides a glimpse into many aspects of their background and history.

Look closely at the present-day country of the Netherlands. This small nation in northwestern Europe is known for many things, including windmills, wooden shoes, and tulips. One-third of its land area actually lies below sea level. This *polder* land was claimed from the seafloor through a complex system of dikes and levees, pumps and canals. The Dutch spent centuries creating new dry land from the seabed. Soon, new agricultural fields appeared as, eventually, did towns and cities.

The Dutch realized that the sea was not an enemy but an opportunity. They began to engage in seafaring. As explorers, traders, and eventually colonizers, Dutch seafarers reached the most remote areas of the globe. In the sixteenth and seventeenth centuries, the Dutch sailed around the Cape of Good Hope and returned with boatloads of spices for the European markets. Unlike the Spanish, they built an empire on economic exchange, rather than military conquest. Ports in the Netherlands, particularly Rotterdam, vastly expanded, and the local economies flourished from the profits the trade generated. Eventually, trade made this very small outward-looking West European country one of the wealthiest nations in Europe and the world. The Dutch had pioneered economic globalization.

Little has changed since then. Today Rotterdam remains Europe's leading seaport. The Dutch people enjoy one of the world's highest incomes and standards of living. In 2009, the country ranked sixth on the global Human Development Index, a measure of human well-being. Dutch cities are burgeoning, and windmills still stand out as lonely sentinels of much of the country's landscape.

Ship cargos, however, are now full of Chinese television units or Japanese cars. The days of the spice trade with the Dutch East Indies are part of history. But the principle of economic activity established long ago has not changed. People do what they know the best, and if smart, they continue with improvements. If they do not pay attention to changes, the world will simply bypass them. The Dutch skillfully recognized their possibilities. They continuously improved their capability and expanded their potential to meet each new challenge. Many other countries showed less flexibility, and their inability to adjust to outside changes serves as one of the main factors in their economic decline.

PRESENT BENEFITS FROM THE COLONIAL PAST

The term "change" means transformation from one stage into another. In terms of global economy, this change began with the Industrial Revolution. Much has been written about the downside, or negative outcomes, of European imperialism and colonialism. But it is important to realize that the colonial experience also brought some positive improvements. In India, for example, the national railroad network is the product of British occupation. Currently it represents the largest employer in the country, with almost a million employees.

Certainly the development of democratic institutions was important. Democratic government in India helped preserve the multiethnic country. India is the world's largest democracy in terms of population. Had the country not been a democracy, it easily could have fragmented into a number of smaller states. Seaports and business centers developed in Mumbai (Bombay), Chennai (Madras), and Kolkata (Calcutta). After the British left in the late 1940s and India gained independence, the economic foundation remained in place. Having a strong British economic system in place gave India a tremendous boost. The country was able to actively participate in economic globalization and take advantage of world markets. With a population of more than one billion people, India has a huge workforce and its economy is rapidly expanding.

Many other countries currently benefit from their former colonial experience. Some, like tiny Singapore, are small. Others are much larger in both population and area. Not all of them, however, struck gold. Who the colonial ruler was played a significant role in a country's postcolonial status and well-being. Some countries fell victim to their colonial past. In much of Africa, for example, adequate infrastructure never was developed. Neither were essential political and social institutions. One of Africa's largest countries, the Democratic Republic of the Congo, covers a huge area with an abundance of potential wealth. Natural resources in the ground and on the surface are immeasurable. Minerals, timber, and so forth wait for extraction. At the same time, the Congolese rank among the world's poorest people. Continuous conflicts, famine, disease epidemics, and political corruption are just some of the reasons for their dire living conditions.

Until the 1960s, Congo was a Belgian colony. The colonial ruler showed little interest in the development of either the infrastructure or stable institutions. Belgium's rulers stripped Congo of many resources. Nearly all of the economic benefits found their way to Belgium. The Congolese themselves gained almost no benefits whatsoever. Most of the colony's people had no formal education. The few cities were designed to serve Belgium's administrative needs or its immediate economic activities. Belgium did not develop a well-integrated economic structure. Congo's people were rural and isolated; the great majority of people were engaged in low-yielding, primitive subsistence farming.

When the Belgians left in 1960, Congo fell under the control of a dictator, Mobutu Sese Seko, more concerned with his own wealth than with the well-being of his people. During the 1990s and early 2000s, millions of Congolese died as the result of wars and a power struggle after the dictator's removal. The situation saw gradual improvement recently, but only in the capital, Kinshasa, and surrounding areas. The troubles continue in the remote and isolated countryside.

ISOLATION VERSUS ACCESSIBILITY

Membership in the global economic community comes with a single requirement. A nation must be of some importance to others as a supplier of goods, consumers, or both. This determines its economic status and potential benefits and hazards for investments. Congo possesses a vast wealth of resources. Its minerals and timber are items that are sought by many international corporations. Yet few corporations are willing to take the risk of investing in the country. Political and security issues create too many problems for investors. They shy away and hope that eventually conditions will improve. Should the situation get better, Congo's economic potential can begin to be

Congo did not benefit from colonization as many other nations did. Instead, it became an underdeveloped country, primed for political instability. *Above*, two women run from crossfire in 2006, during Congo's first democratic elections since achieving independence from Belgium.

realized. For that to happen, however, Congo desperately needs foreign investments. It needs foreign help to build the foundation for development, which, in turn, would then attract more investments. Many poor nations are the victims of such catch-22 situations.

Congo's location also isolates the country from ready access to global markets. What if the Dutch had simply kept planting tulips and never developed ports and global trade linkages? They certainly would have fallen behind the changing world of the sixteenth century. The Netherlands and Congo offer sharp contrasts in historical patterns of development. Understanding these differences gives you a better idea of why uneven global economic development exists.

Nations can be remote and isolated geographically, in terms of their location or culturally. The role of geographic differences has shrunk in recent decades. Larger and faster ships, trains, trucks, and planes have helped to improve transportation. A much better transportation infrastructure also has helped to shorten travel times and to greatly lower shipping expenses. Current markets are well connected. Pipelines and oil tankers satisfy the world's thirst for fossil fuels. The Internet connects once-remote areas in a heartbeat. We have come a long way, from horse-and-buggy travel to geostationary satellite communications in less than a century! Today, distribution of information and goods is fast and reliable. Fiber-optic cables deliver information that, we are told, doubles each year. We now exchange more market data (between producers, consumers, and financial exchanges) in a day than we did in an entire year only several decades ago.

This has prompted some experts to address the issue of a "universal world." After the end of the Cold War, many political and economic barriers fell apart. The Soviet Union disintegrated in 1991. New countries emerged into an era that many people foresaw as one of economic cooperation and progress. They believed that economic globalization would erase distance and barriers. Increased accessibility to the global markets would affect every-

BIG MAC INDEX

One of McDonald's competitors suggests that we should "Think outside the bun." Yet it was exactly the "bun thinking" that prompted the editors of a widely respected weekly magazine, *The Economist*, to introduce the hamburger index as an economic indicator. The Big Mac Index is a clever way of showing the cost of living in various countries. It is based upon the cost of McDonald's popular hamburger from country to country.

The McDonald's franchise, together with the Coca-Cola Company, is a classic example of globalization. It began in California as a family restaurant founded by the McDonald brothers. The idea of fast preparation and serving of meals was bought by entrepreneur Ray Kroc, who kept the restaurant's original name. Today we can see the famous Golden Arches on more than 31,000 restaurants in 119 countries. McDonald's is truly a global franchise.

This is why *The Economist* uses the Big Mac to compare the purchasing power of people in different countries. The Big Mac Index begins with the cost of the sandwich in the United States. It then contrasts the U.S. cost to that of other countries. This allows parallels to be drawn in terms of purchasing power parity (trade of currencies that makes prices of identical goods equal in each country). For example, the American Big Mac may cost $3.00, but in the Eurozone (members of the European Union that use the euro) its value is not identical. If prices in euros, adjusted for difference in dollars, are above $3.00, then currencies of those countries are overvalued (stronger/higher). If the price is less than $3.00, currency is undervalued (weaker/lower) against the dollar. If a single Big Mac costs 3.00 euros, and in reality one euro equals 1.3 dollars, then consumers in the Eurozone pay much more for it.

This index is not a true scientific tool, but it is interesting. Can you imagine paying $5.74 for a Big Mac in Norway or $5.75 in Switzerland? In Mexico, on the other hand, the burger costs $2.36. In Pakistan, it is so inexpensive that if you spent your weekly allowance on Big Macs, you might quickly become sick of the golden arches!

one in positive ways. Increased prosperity that resulted from greater global economic interaction was creating the *flat world.* "Not so fast!" the opposing side said. Cultural differences, they insist, play a much larger role in a country's isolation and accessibility. And ultimately, cultural factors determine the scope of a country's economic position and progress.

REGIONAL DIVERSITY

Culture is the essence of a people's being. Humans are born into many different cultures. As a result, we have quite different norms of social behavior, ethics, religion, and so forth. This is what makes an Indonesian person different than a Norwegian, or a Brazilian different than a Kazakh. Their cultural differences are pronounced, and they affect the economic process in a number of ways. Furthermore, not everyone believes that globalization is the ultimate solution to all of our needs. In fact, it is the argument that globalization destroys cultural identities that stimulates an even stronger grip on one's cultural identity. Some people and countries do not want to conform to the cultural blending that globalization provides. That is, they do not want to be like everyone else. This is true despite the potential economic advantages it offers. They do not want to lose much of their traditional way of life, even if it would mean economic gain.

Scandinavia

On a larger scale, culture in general can affect the economic behavior of an entire country. On a lesser scale, it affects particular establishments and corporate endeavors. Let us illustrate this with several examples of the governance systems in different regions. We begin with the Scandinavian system of cooperation among the government, business, and labor. The general socioeconomic idea in this region is that everyone is working for the common good of their nation. The Scandinavian countries, such as Norway and Sweden, are rather unique in this view. People are able to organize their economic system to support the welfare state and to distribute wealth. But they also willingly share the burden of high taxes necessary to accomplish such goals. In times of economic hardship, the representatives from business, labor, and the government all work together to find solutions.

Scandinavians find this system workable, as is evident in their generally very high quality of life. They enjoy some of the highest standards of living, best formal education, gender equality, and personal liberties. The middle class forms the nations' backbone. Such cultural characteristics are deeply entrenched and unlikely to change in a drastic way. The role of democratically elected officials is to serve the nations' needs. If they fail, they will not be reelected. The final result is that Scandinavians are well immersed into the global economic structure. They welcome globalization, as they harvest the benefits.

The Middle East

Middle Eastern cultures enjoy a model that differs greatly from that of the Scandinavians. Collective organizing in terms of an entire nation's future socioeconomic prosperity is rarely an option. This is particularly true of the region's multiethnic countries. Allegiance to one's ethnic group or tribe is more important than general cooperation for the national well-being. This arrangement opens wide the doors of potential corruption, which, in turn, blocks progress. Different groups eye one another with suspicion. Few governments are freely elected. Most leaders rise to power through violent means. Some follow in the footsteps of previous strongmen who tightly controlled both the government and the economy. They believe their role is to rule, to govern people instead of working for the people. The wealth is unequally spread; most of it is held by a small number of extremely wealthy people, while the majority of the population remains dirt poor.

The rewards of globalization are not reaped by everyone. Despite profitable exports such as oil, great economic disparity persists in areas of the Middle East, where many impoverished citizens live among trash (*above*).

Ordinary people in these countries are used to this system mostly because they have never experienced anything different. The Middle East's history is one of conflict and feuding strongmen who ruled with an iron fist. Individual economic and political rights, such as they exist, are distributed through the state from top to bottom. This is exactly the opposite from the bottom-up system in Scandinavia. It is not surprising that, despite enormous oil revenues, some countries in the Middle East experience perpetual economic hardship. What we in the West see as corruption there is simply a cultural requirement of helping one's kin. Many major economic decisions result from such behavior; to outsiders, they do not make any practical sense. This is why globalization often is perceived as being a destructive force. Its benefits are not harvested by all. Instead, it often appears to ordinary people that the global connections are against their local cultural values. Cultural isolation, then, is favored over accessibility. To expect a sudden cultural leap from the existing views in the Middle East would be premature. It may take many generations for this region to begin resembling Scandinavia. Some scholars, in fact, doubt that it ever will.

Latin America

The final example features Latin America, a region of strong Iberian cultural heritage. Most countries in South America are former possessions of the Spanish kingdom. In macroeconomic terms, that means a similar system was in place throughout the entire region for centuries. In each country, a small number of families held the political and economic power. They owned the land and the capital, and they controlled the government. These families all shared a common European ethnic background that was primarily Spanish (Portuguese in Brazil). Millions of Native Americans of varied ethnic backgrounds remained poor, power-less, landless peasants. As in the Middle East, general coopera-tion never existed.

Social and economic polarization continues to persist throughout much of Latin America even today. Little was done to improve the living conditions of the masses. Wealth remained concentrated in a small number of hands. With grad-ual improvements during recent years, conditions have begun to change. This time the economic shift moved in exactly the opposite direction. With free elections, supporters of the lower class came to power in a number of countries. One-sided politi-cal decisions now often clash with the economic reality. The governments of Venezuela and Bolivia, for example, favor social programs for the poor, despite the fact that they lack funds to support their bold initiatives. Such programs are wildly popular among the lower class (the majority of the voting-age population), even though they can result in long-term economic hardship.

In Latin America, many corporations and other businesses are subject to domestic political maneuvering. Their success or failure is more dependent upon local governmental decisions than it is on national and international market fluctuations. Redistribution of money leads to increased debt to international lenders. This, in turn, can lead to higher taxes and tariffs imposed upon foreign investors. To remain popular at home, with the enthusiastic support of the masses, the governments' unwise measures hurt their global economic status and connections. Instead of fully participating in globalization, they increasingly see it as a potentially destructive force to their so-called reforms. This is why so many Latin American countries experience slow economic development. In terms of policies, many of them pursue "one step forward and two steps backward" policies. Governments (as outgrowths of a culture) can create forceful barriers to long-term prosperity in order to harvest short-term benefits.

CULTURAL BARRIERS AND BUSINESS AS USUAL

The "shrinking Earth," as it applies to economic geography, affords corporations many options. For example, they can move their operations across national boundaries to save on production expenses, which they increasingly do. Relocating from the United States to Canada or Scandinavia generates few difficulties. Business models are similar and people are culturally alike. But elsewhere, there are countless examples of problems that result from economic globalization.

Imagine what can happen when a U.S. corporation opens a branch in India. Can we expect a flawless procedure in a country with an entirely different culture than north European (and its outgrowth Northern American culture)? In the early 2000s, a large American corporation opened a branch in Chennai (Madras), India. It spent more than $50 million in infrastructure development and a worker education program. The purpose of the business was to design and proofread financial documents. The corporation saw this expansion as beneficial in two ways. First, it was affordable because an Indian worker receives a fraction of an American worker's salary. The second reason was the time difference. Chennai is ten time zones away, and Indians work while Americans sleep. Therefore, the business was always open.

MAKING CONNECTIONS

During medieval times, Europeans realized that the world was open for exploration. Until 1492, when Christopher Columbus reached the Americas, Europeans mainly concentrated on finding the shortest routes to various places in the Eastern Hemisphere. One such place was Timbuktu, a city of almost mythical character. It was the center of Saharan trade, where gold, slaves, and salt were among the items exchanged. Far from the reach of any Christian, Timbuktu was located in the heart of Muslim western Africa, in the present-day country of Mali.

Only the stories of its glory reached Europe. When the first European finally entered the city in the nineteenth century, he found a dilapidated and largely forgotten place full of mud (adobe) shacks. There was no visible sign of the city's past glory. What happened to Timbuktu? For centuries, it had served as a key trading center. The city was strategically located. To the north lay the sprawling Sahara Desert, with its parched landscapes and nomadic herders. They controlled the market of precious salt. To the south were the hot, humid lands of West Africa. They offered slaves, gold, and ivory. The environments and people were vastly different. Neither group could function well in the environment of the other.

What appeared as a winning combination at first soon became a growing concern. Several years into the project, the Chennai branch was still lagging in quality of work behind branches in the United States and Europe. The root of the problem was strictly cultural. It had little to do with the willingness of people to work hard. The American managers were completely ignorant of important Indian cultural practices. As a result, they created an unproductive work environment. For example, in India people of higher castes never interact with individuals of lower castes. Yet the American managers grouped people of

Timbuktu was in a position to take advantage of these cultural and environmental differences. The city grew as the region's lead trading center. By the mid–fifteenth century, however, Portuguese mariners reached the southern coast of western Africa. There they were able to trade directly with locals. The trans-Saharan land route was no longer needed. Timbuktu immediately lost the strategic economic significance that its location had created.

Unless they rapidly adjust, many places can lose their status in such a way. Today, more than ever before, the world is experiencing rapid change. In the business world, as elsewhere, it is important to look ahead. Changes in government, economic conditions, and technology, such as transportation and communication, are just some of the things that can impact businesses. Outsourcing, for example, has both positive and negative consequences for all areas involved.

What do you foresee happening to your community during the next several decades? What changes might help, or hurt, your community and its businesses? How do you benefit from outsourcing? Has your community been hurt in any way by economic globalization?

different castes together and forced them to cooperate on equal terms. Workers from the higher castes felt disrespected; those from lower castes were seen as being inferior.

Then the issue of personal space arose. Indians generally require less personal space than do Americans; they like to be close together. The Americans, however, designed and constructed the building with large offices that offered a great deal of personal space. The Indian workers felt isolated and alone, and their productivity suffered as a result. Many other issues surfaced from cultural misunderstanding. Ultimately the company's profit suffered.

Another example is American companies outsourcing their customer service operations to India. As corporations realized how profitable it was to outsource their service branches to the South Asian country, many American offices were closed. Soon, however, important cultural differences between Americans and Indians became apparent. Credit card companies and other financial institutions, in particular, faced a large backlash against outsourcing. Cardholders felt uncomfortable. They were deeply concerned that personal financial information was being given to people in a distant country. It was one thing to ask about an operation manual for a new television set or a computer. It was quite another matter to reveal financial information. The issue of giving jobs to foreigners in a distant land and revealing personal financial information brought a flood of complaints. Many companies had to rethink their actions.

ECONOMIC SYSTEMS

The processes of production and consumption rely on product demand. Distribution issues, too, are generated on the basis of demand. When demand decreases during times of economic hardship, for example, the price of products declines. In order to account for lowering demand, manufacturers have to lower production. This in turn lowers profits and affects future expansion. The end of an economic downturn is signaled by an increase in demand. The American automotive industry provides a good example of this process. Each time the national economy experiences hiccups, the auto industry's profits rapidly decline. Uncertainty keeps consumers from spending, and people choose to hang on to their vehicles for a longer period of time than usual.

In the 2008 economic downturn, the purchase of new vehicles suddenly decreased by 30 to 40 percent. General Motors, Ford, and Chrysler, as well as many foreign carmakers, lost fortunes. The sudden plummet in sales affected salaries, and thousands of layoffs followed. This contributed to the growth of national unemployment rates and negatively affected already shaken stock markets. At the same time, drivers chose to travel less and the price of gasoline decreased. More affordable gasoline prices usually stimulate vehicle sales, but not this time. National economic woes, not the quality of their fleet, brought the automotive industry to its knees. Automakers suffered from being a part of the interconnected national economic system.

Not all economic systems are identical. Their nature and success depend heavily on how the economy is structured and also on the level of development. The postindustrial world is much different than those places where industrial development is not yet established. Some countries focus on specialization in a single aspect of economy, such as farming or mining. Others, like most well-developed countries including the United States and Canada, have extremely diversified economies. And, as noted earlier, economic systems often become victims of ideological decisions that influence their scope and abilities.

There are many economic systems, each of which has its own strengths and weaknesses. Here, some of them are described and illustrated in terms of their main characteristics. All economies are based upon different ways that people produce, distribute, and use goods and services. Attention is also given to the well-being of people involved in each system. How these goals are achieved has varied greatly through time. Huge differences also exist from culture to culture. Originally, all humans practiced a subsistence economy based upon primitive hunting, fishing, and gathering. Much later, perhaps 10,000 years ago, some people began to practice agriculture. Some raised crops, and others herded animals. A few did both. Then, a few centuries ago, things changed dramatically. With the Industrial Revolution, manufacturing, trade, and commerce became widespread. A discussion of these various systems follows, as does a consideration of the different ways in which wealth is distributed.

TRADITIONAL SUBSISTENCE ECONOMIES

In a subsistence economy, people produce only what they need in order to survive. They do not worry about making a "profit." And in most instances, little if any thought is given to "saving" for the future. People practicing a traditional subsistence economy are often said to live a "feast-or-famine" existence. Everyone must contribute in some way to his or her family, clan, or tribe. Those who are unable to do so simply do not survive. Because there is no accumulation of wealth, everyone—at least in an economic sense—is very much alike. There is no social division of "rich" and "poor."

Hunters, Gatherers, and Fishers

Until rather recently in human history, all economic activity was based upon mere subsistence. People hunted and gathered. Some who lived near water fished to provide food for themselves and their families. They used the natural elements in their immediate environment. Stone, wood, and animals were the primary resources used to make their shelter, clothing, tools, weapons, and other material needs.

Some lived a hand-to-mouth, feast-or-famine existence. Others were more fortunate. Edible fruits, nuts, berries, roots, seeds, and other plant parts were abundant. So were animals that could be eaten. Tropics and subtropics, in particular, provided a year-round abundance of food and raw material. This is a major reason why humans occupied these warmer areas of the world for so long. They bartered (traded) for things that they themselves were unable to produce.

Today very few people still live this way. Most of those who do are members of tribal groups that live in very isolated areas. A few, for example, continue to exist in the Amazon Basin, wet tropical portions of Africa, and the islands of Southeast Asia. Until recently, at least, some people of the far north also lived as subsistence hunters and fishers.

Subsistence Agriculture

What social scientists call the Agricultural Revolution began perhaps 10,000 years ago in several places. One early center was Southwest Asia, particularly the area of Mesopotamia in present-day Iraq. Another was Southeast Asia, where early farming was based upon rice cultivation. In the Americas, Mesoamerica (southern Mexico and northern Central America) was an early center of agriculture. So were the central and northern Andean regions. Gradually, through time, the idea of farming and herding spread from these areas to others. By the eighteenth century, most of the world's people practiced subsistence agriculture. Today, hundreds of millions of people in Latin America, Africa, and Asia still do.

The basic premise of a traditional economy is the absence of cash markets and the barter, or trade, of goods and services. Throughout the developing world, many rural people continue to depend upon farming and bartering to make ends meet. It is difficult for us to comprehend that even today, many of the world's people get by on less than a dollar per day. Yet they do, and most of the time quite successfully.

Each morning at the crack of dawn, a tribesman in a village in Laos enters his rice field. His cultivation practices differ little from those of his ancient ancestors. He floods a terraced field with water and plants rice. (Water limits the growth of weeds but does not hurt the rice.) If the growing season is successful, he may have two harvests. If the crop fails, his family may starve. In good years, enough rice is reserved to feed the family. There may even be some left over to exchange for other goods in the local village market. A new hoe, clothes for his children, or a set of wooden bowls is the result of barter between him and his fellow villagers.

Not everyone is growing rice here. Some are blacksmiths who make many things, including agricultural tools. Others are involved in carpentry. They may specialize: one builds beds and another makes boats, which they then barter for rice to feed their

Despite increasing globalization, traditional economies still exist and subsistence farming is practiced in many parts of the world. This Laotian farmer plows a rice paddy by employing the same methods his ancestors did: using a water buffalo and a wooden plow.

own families. Such a system has worked well for centuries. No one in the village seems to worry about the outside world's problems. Life continues pretty much as usual. There are no business offices, universities, or Starbucks. Cash does not buy much here. Most of the villagers are illiterate. There is little need for formal education in order to survive within a traditional system. They learn to live on their own terms.

In a subsistence economy, families often are quite large. Rather than being a "drag" on a family's resources, children make a valuable contribution to their family's economic well-being. From a young age they help the family with work. Youngsters may collect firewood, help clear fields, watch over the family's livestock, fetch water, or do other chores.

In equatorial African villages, conditions are much the same. Instead of rice, peasants grow maize (corn), millet, or cassava. They clear forests by burning trees and shrubs, then plant fruits and vegetables. Soils are of poor quality and have little organic material. Burning the vegetation to clear the field contributes some nutrients. But in a few years, the soil becomes infertile and crops will no longer thrive. The field is abandoned and villagers "slash and burn" another area, then repeat the process. Here, too, agricultural products are exchanged for other necessities. Families are large, and everyone in the village knows his or her role in the tightly knit society.

MARKET ECONOMIES AND CAPITALISM

During the past several centuries, much of the world has experienced an economic boom. Technology has vastly expanded, and the workforce is much better trained. As a result, the production of goods has soared. Trade and commerce have been radically transformed. So have patterns of consumption.

Much of this boom is associated with the Industrial Revolution, which began in Great Britain during the eighteenth century. Development of the steam engine provided a new and inexpensive source of energy. It soon became harnessed to provide power for pumps, mills, and both rail and ship engines. Milling and manufacturing boomed. Factories needed workers, who had to be compensated for their labors. Cities grew around the new factories. Because so many people were working at one task, they required goods and services provided by others. Specialization became widespread. So did the need for some kind of formal education focusing upon the three R's: reading, (w)riting, and (a)rithmetic. These developments were the primary contributors to the development of market economies and capitalism.

During the eighteenth and nineteenth centuries, Western Europe tried a daring experiment. The Europeans began to use banknotes (cash) as a means of paying for goods and services within a capitalist economic system. Governments printed money and attached its value to the amount of available reserves in gold or silver. Depending on the amount and value of money, goods could be produced and purchased. Previously, in subsistence economies, barter had been the means of exchange.

Private enterprise with minimal governmental intrusion was the hallmark of the new process. In this system, an investor, whether individual or corporate, produces or purchases goods and sells them to consumers for a profit. Then the profit is reinvested into another venture. Prices are regulated by the market itself. They are determined on the basis of production and demand. If demand is high and production is low, prices automatically rise. If an overabundance of a product exists and there is little interest in buying it, then prices fall. Capitalism began to flourish during the nineteenth century. Today it is still the backbone of the European and Northern American economies, as well as a number of other strong economies.

Although each nation has a different experience with capitalism, the basic ideas of free market participation are similar. For example, a large retailer purchases orange juice from a corporation that produces and packages it for consumers. The corporation does not necessarily own the orange groves. It may have purchased oranges from growers. By the time we buy the juice, it has passed through several stages of production and distribution. At each stage—from grower to seller—someone made a profit.

If a hurricane hits Florida and destroys an orange grove, the price of orange juice will increase. Demand remains the same because many of us really like to have a glass of orange juice each morning. Yet the availability of oranges has drastically decreased. To meet the demand, companies have to import some juice from abroad, perhaps from Brazil. This increases the transportation cost, for which someone must pay. Therefore, there is a jump in the price we pay for a container of orange juice.

One positive of a free capitalist system is the competition, from which consumers greatly benefit. If the price of a particular product is too high, competitors may take advantage and lower their own prices. New technological developments lower production and distribution costs, which also is reflected in the price of an item. (This is one of the factors that helped make Wal-Mart so successful.) Without competition there is little incentive to improve a product or to control the cost of an item. This is why we have more than a single type of orange juice on our grocery store shelves.

PIRACY ON THE HIGH SEAS

In recent history, piracy on the high seas was pretty much limited to Hollywood movies and Disney theme parks. For most of us, it is something associated with scoundrels like Blackbeard and various others who looted and pillaged their way into history books. However, pirates attacking merchant ships in international waters actually never ended. The old Spanish galleons transporting Aztec and Incan gold are but a distant memory. But today, huge container ships loaded with television sets or automobiles are equally attractive. So are the enormous vessels that transport petroleum.

Global trade has created conditions in which oceanic transportation routes are filled with thousands of ships. During times of peace, they have little or no formal protection against pirates. Caribbean pirates, as movies portray, would seize the ship, take the loot, and spend it on rum and women in one of their hideouts. Today's pirates seize a ship and demand ransom from its owners. The price for release of the ship and its crew is sky high—in the millions of dollars. In previous decades, Southeast Asia was a hotbed of high seas piracy. Particularly dangerous was the narrow Strait of Malacca, located between Malaysia and Indonesia. The region's hundreds of islands provided many places to hide. And the loosely patrolled sea allowed the pirates to roam waters without fear of interference.

How Free Is Free?

In theory, market economies are supposed to operate without government interference, except to prevent fraud and other illegal activities. What this arrangement does is allow everyone to compete fairly, without favors or restrictive barriers. In such conditions, private enterprises flourish. Those who cannot compete make room for those who can. In reality, however, as recent events in the United States have shown, governments often do step in and disobey the rules of a free market. They can intervene in a variety

---

Currently, the waters off the coast of northeast Africa, particularly Somalia, hold the infamous status of being a hotbed of piracy. Most ships prefer to avoid the long route around the southern tip of Africa. They choose to take the Suez Canal, which links the Red and Mediterranean Seas. More than 20,000 ships pass through this narrow waterway each year. Some are military or private, but most are commerce-oriented vessels transporting valuable goods to world markets.

A heated civil conflict rages in Somalia, leaving the country in political and economic disarray. With no stable leadership and few legitimate options to support oneself financially, many people have turned to seizing ships. Modern-day pirates are well-equipped with speedboats, GPS technology, and deadly weaponry. They even managed to take control of a Saudi Arabian tanker loaded with oil worth $100 million!

Once pirates take possession of a vessel, there is little that can be done to prevent them from demanding a ransom. The attacks have become such a nuisance that several countries have sent military units to patrol the waters around Somalia. In 2008, the United Nations took active steps to combat the growing scourge of piracy on the high seas. The UN decided to allow international forces to cross into Somalia's territorial waters and even dry land in pursuit of pirates.

of ways. For example, governments can create central banks that oversee the supply of money to markets. This is the role of the Federal Reserve Banks in the United States. Regulatory actions artificially affect the market, the prices of goods, and the freedom of interaction in long-term ways that can be harmful.

Until the economic crisis of 2008, the U.S. economy was among the world's least regulated capitalist systems. That year the country suffered a major financial crisis. The financial sector failed. The Federal Reserve responded by making a massive infusion of money in order to prevent a meltdown of even the largest banks. In a free market economy, the market regulates prices and purges the system of inefficient corporations. This time, however, the government artificially kept alive underperforming institutions by giving them money. Why, you might ask, is this a problem? The reason is that when more money is put in the system, it often contributes to inflation. That is, the price of consumer products increases, causing a decrease in the value of currency. Orange juice that cost $2.50 soon costs $3.00. With higher costs, your money doesn't go as far. At the same time, individual salaries do not grow at the same rate, which ultimately means the dollar in our wallet is losing its value.

Let's go back to our imaginary Laotian village. Imagine the village elders have a large store of rice reserves. They decide to give the rice to the blacksmiths, who are members of a powerful local clan that supports the elders. The blacksmiths now have enough rice that they do not have to depend upon bartering with other villagers in order to feed their families. Since they now control much of the float of rice prices, the blacksmiths decide to increase their own profits by raising the price of a hoe from 10 to 20 pounds of rice. Farmers who need a new hoe cannot afford one. Without a hoe, they are unable to cultivate their fields. They fall into even greater poverty and perhaps have to sell their land to the blacksmiths. The simple act of village elders giving rice to the blacksmiths changed the balance of the village's economy. It also threatens to destroy the

Senator Charles Schumer and Representative Carolyn Maloney discuss rising food prices in 2008. In 2007 and 2008, food inflation rose considerably, due in part to poor crops and in part to increases in labor costs for the manufacturing and serving of processed foods.

well-being of many less socially and economically powerful village residents.

PLANNED ECONOMIES AND SOCIALISM

The opposite of a free market is a directly controlled economic system. In some countries, the government fully determines the entire economic process. It controls planning, production, distribution, and every other aspect of the national economy. The best example of this approach is the former Soviet Union and other Communist countries. In the West, market forces control economic development. But in the Soviet Union, economic development was controlled by the Communist Party and was dictated from Moscow, the capital. Central economic planning ignored private enterprises and put everything under control of the state.

In such a system, competition does not exist. Orange juice is not produced by a private company; rather, it is produced by a government-operated entity. Prices are predetermined by bureaucrats and are often set artificially low (basic foods) or high (luxury items). Only a single type of orange juice, under a fixed price, can be purchased in the grocery store. The variations are only in the amount of pulp in that juice. Thus, a single government-owned company dominates each aspect of the economy.

Historical evidence points to many shortcomings within such economic systems. The Soviet Union fell apart under its own restrictive and impractical policies. When a single company operates under political guidance, corruption can thrive. There is no interest in expanding business beyond what is officially mandated. This arrangement offers few incentives. Diversification is also a problem. Soviets placed a heavy emphasis on military development. The country's civil infrastructure remained a low priority and suffered accordingly. Also, foreign trade is restricted and must conform to the government's political agenda. This greatly affects those aspects of the economy that rely on the international exchange of goods. This type of trade often involves the trading of items, rather than financial transactions. When this occurs, a chronic absence of cash exists. Soviet tractors, for example, were exchanged for Polish steel even though there was little need for steel at the time. But the tractor company had to follow political directives established by the Communist government.

Communist societies have the most restrictive economic systems. When a government takes charge of economic planning, its decisions can lead to serious social problems. Individual freedoms are the main victims of a government-imposed "common good." Personal choices are allowed only if they fall within the approved framework of governmental policies. People who cannot compete economically become complacent and lose interest in economic progress. This lethargy and its impact upon a country's economy can become a huge problem for society.

MAKING CONNECTIONS

ATTITUDES TOWARD WORK

Attitudes about work differ greatly from culture to culture. Americans are known worldwide as being workaholics. They spend more time engaged in work-related activities than any other developed nation. They also take less vacation time, about ten days a year. Many Europeans take vacations that are twice as long as that of the typical American. Americans, according to a humorous European expression, spend more time preparing for vacation than actually enjoying their time off. Needless to say, few people in other lands admire the American work ethic or would want to exchange work schedules.

Another aspect of the American work ethic is to disallow relaxation at the workplace. In Taiwan, for example, a quick snooze is considered beneficial for worker productivity. Americans also often value cooperative contributions over individual assignments, but not everyone shares those values. Numerous examples illustrate that the changing global economy brings a number of workplace challenges. In the past, this was not much of a problem. But today, when multinational corporations operate across the world, they have to adjust to local cultural requirements.

Managers must understand the needs of their workers whether they are in the United States, India, Egypt, or elsewhere. Yet in each country, the culture imposes its own unique set of values and expectations. The reality is that such diversity will become even more widespread and important in the future. How would you adjust your understanding of other cultures if transferred to Shanghai or Moscow tomorrow? Would you be able to operate in a system entirely different from your own?

Just as in capitalism, the Communist world is diverse and each country has a slightly different approach to handling its economy. Socialism is a milder form of the economic system practiced by Communists (at least in terms of its "pure" form). The basic idea of a government regulating its economy is still there. For this reason we find socialist principles practiced even within some democratic nations. For example, many democratic countries own their own national railway, mining industries, petroleum production, or some other economic activity. They have nationalized certain industries, thereby denying private ownership of these sectors of the economy. In Western Europe, the government may place a single corporation in charge of a particular activity. When this occurs, free market competition is limited or denied.

MEASUREMENT OF WELL-BEING

The ultimate objective of all economic activity is to improve people's quality of life. It can be something as simple as trading a homemade hoe for a bag of rice. For others, it may mean selling television sets and other appliances to accumulate money to buy a vacation house and yacht. To truly measure people's well-being we need to understand the social and cultural context in which they function. Central Asian nomadic herders enjoy what they do. But they have little to show for their efforts other than their horses, sheep, and a few basic necessities. Their economic system of subsistence is as simple as their lives. They make little impact on the surrounding world.

In the industrialized and postindustrial world, we measure everything in dollar terms, including judging individuals and their success in life. Despite its emphasis on materialism, the capitalist system has contributed to vast improvements in the general quality of life. It was responsible for history's fastest gains in overall human well-being. Generated wealth is distributed through society to improve lives across the board. The results are obvious. They include improvements in health, life expectancy, literacy, housing, diets, and countless other areas of our lives.

ECONOMIC SECTORS AND RESOURCE USE

Economic systems—the way countries' economies function—illustrate how particular countries operate internally and as part of global interaction. They do not, however, explain the actual makeup of a country's economy. For that we turn to the study of economic sectors and their role in each nation's economic system. Traditionally, we recognize three main sectors. The primary sector includes agriculture, mining, logging, and fishing. The secondary sector is a domain of manufacturing industries. Services account for the tertiary (third) sector. Depending on the percentage of a country's economy that is dependent upon each of the three sectors, economists are able to judge its economic position relative to that of other nations.

For example, some countries remained predominantly involved in primary industries. Their secondary and tertiary activities were poorly developed. Most people worked in agriculture or were involved in extractive industries. Such lands fall in the category of less developed countries (also called underdeveloped, developing, or third world). Nepal, where more than half the population survives on a subsistence economy, serves as an example of such a country.

If the secondary and tertiary sectors overwhelmingly dominate a country's economy, then it is considered to be developed. Most Western countries fall within this category. Switzerland, for example, is typical of a well-developed nation. The Swiss are recognized leaders in world banking and the manufacturing of luxury goods, such as expensive watches. According to the Human Development Index (HDI), the Swiss enjoy one of the world's highest standards of living. Their income also ranks among the world's highest. The Nepalese, on the other hand, rank near the bottom in both categories.

Traditional divisions, although still rather useful, are falling victim to the changing times. In this chapter we will analyze how global economic interaction and rapid development influence economic sectors and their traditional roles. In light of this transformation, we examine how natural and human (cultural) resources shift their status from sector to sector. The ongoing global technological revolution is the key to this process.

PRIMARY SECTOR

Until the Industrial Revolution, extraction of raw materials and agriculture formed the majority of human economic activity. Services accounted for only a small part of the economy. And for the most part, they were limited to urban areas in an otherwise overwhelmingly rural world. Agriculture was the backbone of economy. A map showing the distribution of the European population during the Middle Ages is revealing. It shows that people were densely clustered in productive agricultural areas. Mining, too, made a significant impact in terms of population distribution. Where accessible minerals existed, people flocked to work in mines. If agriculture and mining were productive, a nation was wealthy. Miners extracted coal and iron and sent it to nearby cities. Forests provided building materials. Fields of wheat, corn, barley, or some other grain fed the citizens. Rural people survived on subsistence methods.

When the Industrial Revolution began in the eighteenth century, previously wealthy areas began to fall behind. Mining and agriculture were no longer the focus of economy. Rather, they became simple suppliers of basic products to urban manufacturing plants and populations. Their significance fell, as did the prices of their products. Technological improvements in production and transportation made everything less expensive. Railroads were able to connect previously remote places and bring inexpensive materials for processing. The primary sector lost influence and status as the world bypassed it in a giant economic leap forward.

During the twentieth century, primary economic activities sharply declined in their relative importance to other economic sectors. By the end of the century, only about 10 to 15 percent of the workforce in developed countries was engaged in primary activities. In the United States, for example, agriculture employs less than 1 percent of the workforce. By comparison, in poorly developed Afghanistan, more than 90 percent of the workforce is engaged in primary economic activities, such as farming or herding.

American Example: Part One

Soon after gaining its independence, the United States entered the nineteenth century as a rural nation. Besides several urban areas in the Northeast, such as New York and Boston, most of the country was rural. The economic focus was on the South and its agriculture, where cotton was the king. In Kentucky, fields of tobacco and corn provided the basis for cigars and whiskey. It looked as though the South had a very strong hand to play in the economic card game.

Yet, by the end of the nineteenth century, much of the South had become an unproductive rural backwater. What happened?

The North was becoming heavily industrialized. Coal mines opened in Kentucky and West Virginia, but they only provided raw materials for booming northern manufacturing cities. Overall development lowered prices of production and distribution of raw materials and foodstuffs. Many Southerners left their homes to seek employment in the booming northern industrial centers. As the North developed economically, the South seemed to decline at a comparable rate. Overall, the spectacular rise in secondary industries catapulted the United States to the status of the world's leading economy. Regional differences remained unfavorable for southerners. For a number of complex reasons, it was very difficult for the South to make the jump from a primary economy to a secondary economy. As a result, southern states continued to struggle. The region experienced decades of social and economic polarization, economic stagnation, unemployment, and growing poverty.

SECONDARY SECTOR

During the nineteenth and much of the twentieth century, those countries with a strong manufacturing sector prospered. Initially, Western Europe and the United States benefited the most. Soon, however, their impact reached out to other lands. Secondary economic activities involve the processing of raw materials into finished products. Examples include refineries, light and heavy industries, textile factories, and various mills. Infrastructure development, such as all types of transportation, construction industries, and the production and distribution of energy, is also part of the secondary sector.

It was widely recognized that the faster countries transformed their economies, the sooner they would benefit. Japan followed that advice. The island nation joined the group of developed nations shortly after World War II. The Soviet Union and other Communist countries tried to follow the American and Western European expansion models. Later on, the Chi-

In 2009, several U.S. steel makers filed a complaint against Chinese corporations, accusing them of flooding the market with steel pipes whose manufacturing had been supplemented by the Chinese government. China has surged ahead of much of the rest of the world in relatively little time to become a major player on the world market.

nese joined the trend, knowing that they too had to catch up with the developing world. Today China is a modern-day poster child of success. The country's growing economy has driven up the price of oil, steel, and many other materials on the global market.

It is difficult and costly to expand a country's secondary sector. Raw materials and natural resources must be purchased. Factories must be built. Transportation networks must be built or expanded to move people and materials from place to place. Workers must be trained. All of these developments require capital resources: money, and lots of it. This is why it is so difficult for many developing nations to build a strong manufacturing base. A steel mill in a remote corner of Africa has little future if a majority of people barely survive on subsistence farming. Yet tradition held that economic development must follow established stages. Thus, if a country was to prosper, it had to move from primary to secondary industrial development. If it worked for the developed nations, it had to work for developing nations as well. Few, however, anticipated that globalization would change the rules of the game and trump conventional wisdom.

AFGHANISTAN'S OPIUM PRODUCTION

Afghanistan is one of the unluckiest places on our planet. Some call it the land of perpetual conflict. Its recent history certainly suggests that this description is realistic. Civil wars and foreign interventions have brought devastation to one of the world's poorest nations. Millions of refugees from Afghanistan now live in camps in Pakistan and Iran. Despite the presence of NATO troops, conditions are far from stable. Much of the countryside, in particular, is a wild and lawless land. Most ordinary Afghans, however, live in the countryside, where they follow a way of life unchanged for centuries. They live in small villages, clustered together for protection. They practice subsistence farming to keep from starving. Tribal relationships provide the major social linkages beyond that of family.

People have to rely on their own ingenuity, as social services are mainly nonexistent. There are few schools, most roads (where they exist) are unimproved, and health care is scarce. Warlords from the ranks of tribal leaders control a good portion of Afghanistan. Their words and actions are the law of the land. The price for going against the demands of the established system may be one's life.

Among the demands is to grow poppy seeds instead of food crops. Through this process, a peasant farmer from rural Afghanistan, who

TERTIARY SECTOR

Today, most of the world's countries no longer depend upon primary or secondary industries as the foundation of their economy. Rather, they have turned to providing many kinds of services. This change has been the key to growing prosperity in many lands. A service-based economy has many advantages. People, for example, rather than natural resources and raw materials, become the primary source of wealth. And what is being exchanged—information, education, health care, entertainment,

---

perhaps has never left his village, contributes to a global-scale economic process. This practice is of course the production and transportation of opium and heroin, illegal drugs manufactured from poppy seeds.

Afghanistan is currently the world's largest contributor of poppy seeds destined for illegal drugs. Returns on manufactured products are measured in billions of dollars. At the end of the route, the drugs reach buyers worldwide and the Afghan farmer eventually harvests the benefit of this year's growing cycle. The following year, he plants and harvests again. He is unaware of other options.

The transition from traditional folk culture to contemporary popular culture, from agriculture to the industrial age, leaves no options to many who have little to bargain with. Subsistence farmers across the globe are in the most difficult position. Most of them must rely on outside forces to determine their future. When, in rare instances, authorities raid fields covered with poppies, they burn them. The farmers' lands once raised crops of grain and other food items. When their crop of poppies is destroyed, what options are left to them to feed their families? They have become helpless victims of addictions, as well as values and laws, in distant lands.

or some other service—does not depend upon a traditional costly infrastructure. The tertiary sector relies on the distribution of already existing products and services. A high percentage of the service sector in a country's economy indicates a well-developed and, frequently, postindustrial nation (one that no longer depends upon manufacturing industries).

Microsoft provides a good example of how the service sector differs from primary or secondary industries. The huge software company began as a hobby and evolved into a billion-dollar corporation in a period of only several years. Bill Gates, the founder, and his associates did not own property or the means to produce or manufacture goods. What they did have was an *idea* of how to provide a service and reap immediate benefits.

In the early days of the information revolution, computer hardware was manufactured by giants like IBM. The actual machines were expensive to produce because of the high cost of their physical components. IBM's management concentrated on controlling the process of production and sale of computers by focusing on hardware, which at that time was profitable. They spent little time thinking about the future of software and simply outsourced it to other companies. One of those companies was Microsoft. In need of a software operation system, IBM entered into an agreement with Microsoft to provide the software. The ultimate outcome of this arrangement was that Microsoft's profits soared, and IBM's fortunes stagnated. Bill Gates simply acquired the software from another firm for an affordable sum and sold it to IBM. He used knowledge to provide a service and to generate profit. This act, however, increased the market visibility of Microsoft as a successful software manufacturer. In the following years, as production costs decreased, the price of hardware plummeted, but prices of software remained high.

As you read these lines, ask yourself how this book could have been produced at a reasonable cost without computer software. The final product in the publishing world is the result of cooperation among many different service providers: writers, editors, proofreaders, printing offices, and many others—all of them dependent upon computer software. Consulting companies are another example of service providers. Their sole purpose is to advise corporations or governments about investment opportunities and operational strategies. Then there are accounting corporations that concentrate on "number crunching" to fulfill tax requirements. Within the tertiary sector, the most important investment is in human capital—the knowledge, skills, and efforts of a labor force. Workers within this sector must be well educated in order to compete in a so-called white-collar job environment.

American Example: Part Two

History sometimes repeats itself. First it was the South that lagged economically as the North shifted from primary industries to the secondary economic sector. Northeastern cities such as Pittsburgh, Cleveland, Detroit, and Buffalo blossomed at that time. Each year new cars were rolling out of automobile plants in Detroit, displaying the greatness of American industrialization. The Interstate Highway System, approved by President Dwight D. Eisenhower in the 1950s, became the world's largest network of highways. In the late 1960s, Japanese automobile manufacturers entered the American market with small compact vehicles and received a laughable response. No one could compete with Americans, critics argued, as they were the leaders.

Then times changed, and the golden days of American manufacturing hit a barrier. What was cutting edge one day became outdated soon after. The tertiary sector took over, and suddenly California became the nation's economic leader. Once booming cities of the Northeast fell into urban decay. Countless corporations and millions of people fled the "Rust Belt" for the warmer climates of the southern and southwestern "Sun Belt." Economically, much of the Northeast fell into despair, as the South had a century earlier. The new age of a service-oriented economy had arrived, and the old winners became new losers. The rest of the world was watching and learning from the American experience.

SKIPPING A STAGE

Global connections continuously change. Those able to ride the coattails on the upswing of progress benefit the most. Many business-oriented people in developing nations realized that international development could serve them much better if they defied some of the conventional thinking. Rather than seeking to develop in a primary-secondary-tertiary fashion, their goal was to leap directly from the primary to the tertiary phase. They realized that if they attempted to develop the secondary industries, they might never catch up with the wealthy nations. They were right.

By skipping a stage, they were able to greatly hasten development. Why, for example, does an African country need a conventional ground-based telephone network? To establish such a network, costly infrastructure must be constructed. It costs much more to build a network of poles and wires than to construct a mobile network. Cellular phones allow users to utilize Internet-based services as well. Communication technology plays a vital role in helping a country make the transition from a primary economy to a tertiary economy. The main reason lies in the affordability of equipment and the ease of its use.

Just over a century ago when Dr. David Livingstone, the first European to venture deep into the heart of Africa, arrived there, local residents had no written language. Today they can communicate with anyone around the globe. Even the local coffee bean farmer in Rwanda can walk to the village or town nearby and check commodity market prices. His plantation is not a subsistence farm anymore, and his coffee is considered a luxury product in the West.

The farmer will earn a good income (by local standards) just to grow coffee for fair-trade merchants in the United States.

A Rwandan coffee farmer shows off his recently-harvested red coffee cherries in 2004. Where once the Rwandan farmer only would grow enough for himself and perhaps for local trade, he now grows enough to be a player on the global market.

He does not have to worry about building the coffee roasting and packaging plant, which the government cannot afford anyway. This part of the process is taken care of by the American corporation that sells the coffee to consumers. When business picks up, more and more farmers will join together and form a body of producers that can negotiate better trade contracts. A local cooperative is formed. It reinvests profits in new land and can employ more people. If everything goes as planned, the original farmer is now having someone else work for him. His children are now in school and soon may be in college. They will return with new ideas about how to succeed in the expanding global system.

In a western African war-torn country, an educated person returns from studies in Europe and is willing to find employment. The war nearly destroyed the country's economy, and it may take years to rebuild factories. Employment is difficult to

MAKING C⊕NNECTI⊕NS

THE "GOOD OLD DAYS"

For most people, wealth creates conditions for a better quality of life. Expanding economy means better housing, food, schools, and health care. It also means more leisure time, recreation, and entertainment. Because of economic and technological developments, food costs less today (as a percentage of income) than ever before. Ask your grandparents how often they enjoyed restaurant meals or could afford fresh fruits and vegetables during the winter months. Only a couple of generations ago, many people in today's developed countries could not afford to eat meat every day.

Throughout the world, many people are still hungry. Their daily economic activity is preoccupied with trying to provide enough to feed themselves and their children. They are unable to afford adequate medical care. As a result, the life expectancy of native peoples in some parts of Africa, Asia, or Latin America is far below life expectancy in the developed world. Imagine tribes in South America's Amazon rain forest. For thousands of years, they survived as hunters and gatherers. Then modernization arrived. In only a couple of decades, their world changed fundamentally. They have options. In order to "make something of their lives" in a modern sense, they must give up their traditional culture. Or they can retain their age-old way of life and become living human relics in a remote village. Most tribesmen in this area die young from diseases and improper medical care. Which option would you choose? What are some of the advantages or disadvantages of your choice?

find even for educated individuals. Then, with help from his European connections, the entrepreneur realizes that there is a blessing in disguise. Cheap land and labor and a favorable climate offer excellent conditions for growing roses. Capital to get a rose farm going is obtained from foreign investors. Soon, roses are being shipped by air to European markets twice a week. The roses, just like Rwandan coffee, are a luxury product now being grown in Africa by African workers. Most importantly, profits stay in Africa and are reinvested in other aspects of local businesses. A plane that delivers roses to Europe now returns with a shipment of other goods to be sold in African markets. Times when the only planes to land were full of military equipment for yet another coup are a distant memory.

Generate Wealth by Skipping a Stage

Perhaps the best example of smart choices in the global environment is the small emirate of Dubai. As one of the United Arab Emirates, Dubai was fortunate to enjoy a high income from oil extraction in the Persian Gulf region. But Dubai is also territorially small and has a limited amount of oil. It is only a matter of time before oil revenues vanish. A careful plan had to be devised in order to avoid almost certain economic hardship. Dubai's leaders knew what the consequences would be. Their country had been dirt poor before the stroke of good luck in the form of oil.

It made no sense to turn this small nation into a manufacturing center. Instead, Dubai chose to invest its wealth in communications, banking, and tourism, pouring billions of dollars into a variety of projects. With careful investments, it became the banking and investment center of Southwest Asia and a global communication hub. Rather than waiting for oil revenues to dry up, Dubai wisely invested in its own future. Its own people benefit greatly from its farsighted developments. So do many other countries that can learn from the example set by this small desert nation.

HUMAN RESOURCES

Population growth is good for the economy of any country and for the global economic system as well. Ultimately, humans are the most valuable resource. Investment in formal education is the best investment that any country can make. A list of the world's leading economies (on a per capita basis) and other data can be revealing. Countries such as Japan, Singapore, the Netherlands, Norway, and Iceland have few natural resources or raw materials. Yet, most of their residents are very well educated. The primary source of domestic wealth is human knowledge and skill—the application of human resources.

Some countries grow increasingly alarmed over a sharp decline in their birth rates. Japan and many European countries already face critical labor shortages because of aging populations and low birth rates. This demographic trend is a reality in all postindustrial nations. Overpopulation prophecies of the 1960s failed to consider the fact that increases in population during agriculture-to-industrialization transformation were only temporary. The population growth–economic growth question is complex and controversial. Some suggest that if a country is to progress economically, its population policies should not be restrictive. Otherwise the need for labor, particularly educated labor, may turn into a major economic problem. Surprisingly, perhaps, because of qualified labor shortages, particularly engineers, even China faces serious difficulties in future economic development. Dubai, too, must rely on immigrant labor to satisfy basic needs in construction and service. Numerous examples from other parts of the world support the notion that humans are indeed the most viable resource. If a country is satisfied with subsistence farming as its economic backbone, then few have to worry about educating residents. That, of course, is not a current global trend. Everyone wants the quality of life the developed world enjoys.

ENERGY
CONSUMPTION

Energy is the driving force of the global economy. It serves as a foundation for initial development and expansion. Fossil fuels, in particular, are essential to this process. The backbone of the Industrial Revolution was the use of coal. Since then, oil has taken over the primary spot, although coal still ranks high in terms of consumption. Nuclear energy became an obvious alternative to fossil fuels during the mid–twentieth century. Its negative image, however, contributed to slow expansion as safety concerns grew over the fear of radiation. During recent decades, alternative energy initiatives have been in the spotlight. They include use of wind and solar energy, as well as various hydroelectric options, such as harnessing tides and waves.

Transitions from one source of energy to another have everything to do with affordability. If buyers believe it is too expensive, then a new type of energy will not be widely accepted. If, however, technology improves, then the new energy source becomes less costly to extract or produce. It then becomes more affordable and enters the global marketplace as a new energy option. One of the main reasons why environmentally friendly alternative energy is developing slowly is because of its cost. Also, sometimes political issues overshadow logical reasons. In the United States, for example, one state may lobby Congress to support specific energy-related regulation. If that state is California, a powerful factor in American politics, one can expect regulation to pass. If, however, it comes from a state with a much lower population and less political "clout," its chances of passing are slim.

Geopolitical factors play a vital role in worldwide energy affairs. The Organization of Petroleum Exporting Countries (OPEC) is an international cartel whose decisions affect the global prices of oil. OPEC and other exporters of oil, such as Russia, reap enormous benefits from traditional energy. Therefore, they have little interest in the development of alternative options. For this reason, the production and distribution of fossil fuels still forms the backbone of the changing global economy. Prices and flow of oil determine rate of development. Affordable prices of oil drive national economies into faster development. High prices eventually cause a slowdown as affordability becomes an issue. This chapter focuses upon a number of economic crises. Let's begin with an analysis of energy's role in the dynamics of the global system.

FOSSIL FUELS

The reason why fossil fuels remain the most popular source of energy is quite simple. Coal, oil, and natural gas are cheap. Yes, as hurtful as it is to pay $4.00 (at its peak) per gallon of gas, this is still a very affordable and efficient source of energy. Fossil fuels are not too difficult or costly to extract and distribute to markets in large quantities. We must understand that fossil fuels drive more than just our cars. They produce energy that powers most industries. They generate most of our electricity. And they are used in the manufacture of many products. Coal alone has more than 100,000 uses! Without oil we cannot build roads on which to drive. Without coal we would freeze during winters and gasp for cool air during hot summers.

Coal

Many people do not like using coal, which pollutes the environment. They want to replace it with clean-burning energy alternatives. Nuclear power is one option, although currently it is even less popular than coal. Rarely do advocates of such proposals realize how important coal is to the global economic system. Today, no alternative energy source can come close to matching the amount of energy created from coal.

Half of American electricity comes from coal-burning power plants. Electricity for business, residential, and public use is delivered through grids connected to these plants. Many other countries depend even more upon coal as their primary energy source. The rapidly emerging Chinese economy is almost exclusively dependent on coal. China must import most of its petroleum, but the country has vast coal reserves. Coal has fueled much of China's recent economic boom. Two-thirds of the country's electricity is produced by coal-burning plants. India also has greatly increased its coal production to help fuel its expanding economy. China, India, and the United States share almost half of the world's coal reserves. The United States alone holds 27 percent of proven world reserves.

According to various estimates, existing coal reserves can continue to satisfy demands for perhaps two centuries. The almost certain discovery of new coal reserves will ensure that the world will not run out of supplies for some time. Certainly alternative resources will be discovered long before coal supplies are depleted. After all, we did not introduce oil because the world ran out of coal.

Oil and Natural Gas

Oil has been used for only about 150 years. The first well was drilled in northwestern Pennsylvania in 1859. Once it did become widely used, however, it played a very important role in international economic development. This is particularly true in regard to transportation. By 1900, extraction methods had improved. Around the same time, the automobile was replacing the horse as the primary means of transportation. The importance of oil and gas increased tremendously with the onset of the automotive age. During the twentieth century, much of the world's industrial development depended upon oil.

The global distribution of petroleum deposits tends to be highly concentrated. Initially, the United States had extensive supplies of oil. This helped the country rise to become the world's leading economic and military power during the twentieth century. Today, Southwest Asia holds about 50 percent of known

Coal is transported by truck in northwest China in 2009. China's new economy depends heavily on coal. The pollution caused by combustion of that coal contributes to nearly half a million deaths per year and poses a threat to the global environment.

petroleum reserves. Russia is in second place, with perhaps 15 percent of proven reserves. Nigeria, Venezuela, and Mexico are also significant producers.

Unfortunately, most of the world's petroleum production does not occur in places where this essential resource is needed. Primary markets are the United States, Western Europe, and Japan. Recently, demand has grown rapidly in China and India because of their booming economies. Each of the foregoing locations has very limited domestic production. They must import most if not all of their oil from areas of production often located thousands of miles away. The imbalance between production and consumption is astonishing. Oil is by far the most important player on the global commodity markets. The United States alone consumes 25 percent of the world's energy. The country's economy depends very heavily upon imported oil and natural gas. This helps to explain why American political leaders—Republicans and Democrats alike—are particularly sensitive to geopolitical issues in Southwest Asia. Unfortunately, this oil-rich region is among the most volatile corners of the world. Conflicts there can greatly upset the global oil supply and the worldwide economic dependence upon this energy source.

Oil prices often are artificially adjusted to account for potential disruptions in supply. The Persian Gulf is the world's primary shipping source for petroleum. Its narrow 20-mile (32-kilometer) opening to the Indian Ocean is a strategic waterway, the Straight of Hormuz. Through this waterway pass huge tanker ships that carry about one-third of the world's oil supply to markets around the globe. Japan, in particular, is dependent upon petroleum from the Persian Gulf region. When Iraq invaded and occupied Kuwait in 1990, Japan provided much of the financial support for the military effort that drove Iraqi forces out a year later.

Oil from the gulf is of good quality and easy to extract. Drilling here is less complicated than in frigid northern Alaska, remote Siberian outposts, or the deep seabeds of the North Sea, Gulf of Mexico, or elsewhere. By the 1960s, shipbuilders began to construct huge supertankers able to carry vast amounts of oil to refining facilities in importing countries. Most Russian oil and gas, and some Asian oil, reach European markets through a network of pipelines. Most of America's oil imports arrive by oil tanker. The crude oil is refined at sprawling plants along the Mississippi River in southern Louisiana and the Texas Gulf Coast.

New Approaches to Extraction

Alternative methods of oil production are becoming more attractive as technology improves. Currently, most extracted oil is in fluid form. But some of the largest remaining deposits are trapped in soil and sands. Until recently, it was too expensive to extract petroleum from oil (tar) sands. During the past decade, however, the price of oil spiked. With the potential to make a profit, many companies invested in the development of this new fuel source. Canadian companies have revolutionized the process of extraction from oil sands. The cost of oil from oil sands is about US$40 per barrel. Anything above that is clear profit.

Canada's Alberta Province is a leader in oil-sand development and production. The Athabasca oil sands basin in northeastern Alberta alone contains as much oil as the rest of the world's proven reserves combined! Canada is the leading supplier of oil to the United States market, and the current rates will more than likely increase. Although oil-sand deposits exist in the United States, environmental and political issues create barriers to their extraction. In Colorado, for example, huge amounts of oil could be extracted from oil shale on federal lands. But many people strongly oppose their development. Exploitation would involve the strip removal of overlying layers of rock. This kind of extraction, critics argue, would permanently scar the environment and destroy valuable natural habitats.

Today, more than ever before, the rapidly changing global economy relies on factors that are independent of usual market forces. In most developed countries, for example, the public is quite sensitive to the importance of protecting the natural

MAKING C⊕NNECTI⊕NS

GETTING AROUND

Urban sprawl—the spread of huge megacities over vast areas—creates many challenges. One of the most difficult is creating an adequate transportation network. If an economy is to thrive, people and materials must be moved rapidly and efficiently. In the United States, ample space in which to grow has allowed cities to expand for decades. Some American metropolitan centers cover a greater area than do some countries! Such conditions create huge difficulties in building a transportation network that is adequate and at the same time affordable to maintain.

A freeway system requires constant expansion in order to connect suburbs with downtowns. Worldwide, most cities were designed before the automobile. Streets are narrow and winding. Most American cities (except in the East) grew after the dawn of the automotive age. Streets are wider and most are straighter than in many other countries. U.S. cities often lack a well-organized and efficient public transportation network. Today, costs for building such a system can run in the billions of dollars. Think about your neighborhood. Can you walk or ride a bicycle to work or to the nearest school, grocery store, or movie theater?

Developing countries battle an opposite problem. The Chinese, for example, never expected an urban boom and the growing prosperity that would allow millions of people to own the new status symbol—an automobile. Traffic jams and gridlocks are choking urban transportation in Beijing and other cities of the developing world. The presence of so many vehicles also contributes to a huge increase in air pollution. Such problems and benefits are the result of globalization and its economic developments. How would you approach the task of planning improvements in the transportation network of the city you know best?

environment. They place a greater value on the natural environment than they do on exploiting its natural economic resources.
This, in turn, contributes to an increase in the cost of resources.
For example, depending upon location, American gas stations
have very different mixtures in their tanks. Gas stations in
Atlanta, Georgia, for example, must follow different state and
local regulations than those in Chicago or Los Angeles. In order
to comply with local laws, fuel might have to be purchased from
a distant refinery, even though a refinery may be operating next
door. Cleaner-burning gas is mandatory in California, for example, but not in many other states. All this factors into the final
price we pay at the station.

When unusual events interrupt distribution, the consequences
are painful. In 2008, after Hurricane Ike ravaged the Texas Gulf
Coast, all oil facilities in the region shut down their production
for a period of time. Distribution from local refineries ceased to
such a degree that many gas stations in Georgia and elsewhere
in the Southeast ran out of gas. Why in Georgia, you may ask? It
was because regulatory measures required that specific gasoline,
produced only in Texas, be imported to the Atlanta area. Although
the other states were in a position to lend gasoline to Georgia, the
gas did not meet local standards. At the same time, the price of
oil was reaching historical highs in prices up to $147.00 per barrel.
Georgians paid a high price in money and their nerves.

ALTERNATIVE FUELS

Environmental concerns and regulation stimulate development
of alternative energy resources. Developed economies have the
financial resources to afford the luxury of a clean environment.
Poorer countries that are in the process of developing can not.
This is why developed nations lead the path in changing international attitudes toward energy use. Huge wind farms dominate
landscapes in many states, including California, Texas, and
Minnesota. Wind is a free and clean natural resource. It can be

Will wind power—a free, effective, clean source of energy—become more widely used around the world, as it is in Denmark (*above*)? While the issue of alternative energies would seem to be free of debate, it is mired in political feuding and public perception.

harnessed to generate electrical power used by industries, businesses, and private residences. In agricultural areas, farmers continue to cultivate the land around the windmills, therefore harvesting double profits.

Some European countries, such as Denmark, acquire much of their energy through windmills scattered in the North Sea. Iceland, a small island nation in the North Atlantic, has developed geothermal energy as an alternative to fossil fuels. The sun's energy is captured by panels in areas where weather permits long periods of clear skies. Hydrogen-powered vehicles are no longer limited to the world of science fiction. These and perhaps other types of fuels are expected to replace petroleum in the not-too-distant future.

THE "FORGOTTEN" ALTERNATIVE FUEL

In times when American dependence on foreign energy supplies is a matter of continuous debate, one alternative fuel option remains in the shadows. This fuel is a naturally growing plant: hemp. Just like corn or any other crop, hemp can be planted and harvested. It has many uses, including conversion to fuel. It has a very strong fiber, well suited for the making of rope. In construction it can provide additional support to concrete. The textile industry uses hemp to improve the strength of clothing. Its seeds are valuable, too, and can be made into healthy oil for domestic use.

More than half a century ago, Henry Ford designed a vehicle with a body made from hemp. Ford was a strong supporter of hemp's use in the automotive industry. He proved that hemp-made vehicles were less apt to be damaged in an accident than those built from traditional materials. If Ford's suggestions had been adopted by the automobile industry, vehicles would be more sturdily built and less expensive than they are today. Cleaner-burning hemp-based ethanol could greatly reduce our dependence upon gasoline. The landscape of the Midwest is dominated by fields of corn and soybeans. Hemp is nowhere to be found, despite its amazing industrial potential. Ford's attempts never saw the light of day in terms of commercial production. Why?

Around the world, industrial production of hemp is increasing. But this is not the case in the United States, where it is illegal to grow the plant. Yet, ironically, the United States is the world's largest importer of hemp! The country outlawed the growing of hemp during the 1930s because some varieties are used for the illegal drug marijuana. Industrial hemp is a different variant that, through genetic engineering, has lost its ability to be used for marijuana. This is why other countries did not ban the production. Those who support the industrial use of hemp blame powerful oil and steel lobbies for the laws that make hemp growing a criminal act.

Current energy demands are too great to be satisfied with alternative energy sources at the present time. The United States alone has a population of about 310 million people. It would take several million towering windmills to produce enough electricity to provide power for their homes. Several million more towers would be needed to produce enough energy to power the country's businesses, industries, and other facilities. Wind farms—with their huge towers and churning blades—are a blight on the landscape in the eyes of many people. When built, a network of transformers and power lines must link areas of production to consumers. This, too, contributes to landscape blight. In most countries, fossil fuels continue to account for more than 90 percent of all energy consumed. During recent years, the high price of oil has forced policymakers worldwide to look for alternatives. A growing number of them are beginning to rethink their previous position on nuclear energy.

NUCLEAR STRATEGY

Nuclear power plants, under normal conditions, do little to pollute or otherwise change the environment. And they are capable of producing vast amounts of electricity. But many people remain skeptical of nuclear-generated energy. The biggest problem facing nuclear power for peaceful purposes is its public image. People worry about the consequences if something goes wrong. They still remember two widely publicized events. In 1979, an accident occurred at Pennsylvania's Three Mile Island nuclear plant. It was followed in 1986 by a terrible incident at the (then) Soviet Chernobyl facility, in Ukraine. Both events could have resulted in unimaginable, worldwide catastrophes. A second major issue is how to store the spent fuel, which is radioactive. It can be stored safely. But transporting radioactive waste from its point of origin to its place of storage raises many safety concerns.

American public support for nuclear energy soured after the Three Mile Island plant near Pennsylvania's capital, Harrisburg, experienced problems. No lives were lost and no major contamination resulted from the event. Nonetheless, widespread fear over what *could* have happened caused many Americans to lose confidence in nuclear plants. In fact, since Three Mile Island, not a single nuclear plant has been built in the United States.

When the Chernobyl nuclear plant in the former Soviet Union experienced an explosion, the traditionally secretive Soviets tried to cover up the event. Some time passed before the public was alerted and an evacuation was begun. Because of political indifference, many lives were lost and considerable environmental contamination occurred. Radioactive fallout from the explosion spread from Ukraine northwestward, as far as Scandinavia. As a result of this accident, some European countries turned away from nuclear energy. Italy, for example, has no nuclear plants. Others remained confident in their technology and ability to build safe facilities. France is one such country. It is the world leader in nuclear-produced electrical energy. More than 70 percent of the country's electricity comes from nuclear plants.

Today, international public opinion is more supportive of nuclear energy. The quality of buildings and equipment has increased greatly. So has the technology needed to run a plant safely. Many new safeguards have been developed that can prevent potentially hazardous accidents. Even most Americans now realize that nuclear energy is perhaps the best alternative to fossil fuels.

The Chinese, in particular, have grandiose plans for the development of nuclear energy. In order to expand economic growth and meet future energy demands, they plan to build more than 100 nuclear power plants across the country. It will take several decades to meet their goal. But China's ambitious goal does point to a major change in the way people think about their energy needs and how these needs can be met.

ECONOMIC CRISES

When times are good, everyone cashes in. An entrepreneur in Silicone Valley collects billions for his innovative business skills. Investors in financial markets harvest the benefits of a growing economy. Paper millionaires even pop up in the middle class as their investments grow. A cup of coffee in a specialty shop can cost $5.00, yet the demand keeps growing. People have money and are not afraid of spending it. Starbucks, the leading corporation in the latte-preparing world, continuously builds new stores. Its major competitors also grow.

This comes as good news for our coffee farmer in Rwanda. Demand for his coffee beans is increasing. He expects his annual profit to increase by several thousand dollars, a drastic change by local standards. With the profits, he can further expand. Several more fields will be cultivated. And a dozen unemployed peasants will be hired to work the new land. An Italian who makes deluxe coffee machines for American coffee stores expects profits in the millions. A Chinese manufacturer has received an order to increase production of paper cups and their plastic covers. Starbucks expects higher consumption, therefore higher sales, and needs more cups. Positive news triggers a rise in the company's stock price as investors begin to pour in. Rather than walking barefoot, several dozen Rwandan farm workers now can buy shoes manufactured in Southeast Asia. The global connections are well established, and everyone is satisfied. A cup of coffee is truly the product of many global connections!

THE TURNAROUND

Seemingly overnight, the good fortune described above comes crashing down. The changing global economy suddenly makes a U-turn on the highway of growth. In times past, most economic crises affected only local areas. If Latin America was affected, for example, other regions would continue without experiencing too much distress. Today, however, economic crises do not recognize political boundaries. A problem in one location can spread like wildfire to places around the globe. When American consumers, for example, begin to tighten their financial belts, they can start a chain reaction. African farmers, coffee brokers, Chinese manufacturers, and dozens of others who in any way depend upon coffee begin to feel the pressure.

Instead of buying a single latte at Starbucks for $4.00, a consumer buys a pound of coffee for $8.00 and makes his own brew at home. Rather than getting two cups for $8.00, he is able to make several dozen cups. As demand drops, so do the profits of Starbucks. The sharp drop in demand strikes African growers particularly hard. Growers can hardly make ends meet, and they can no longer hire the additional help. Although the foregoing examples are fictional, they closely match reality. When the economic crisis of 2008 began, Starbucks's profits plummeted 97 percent in just a short period of time. The corporation had to close many stores. And its stock dropped in value by more than half, resulting in losses to tens of thousands of investors.

The Starbucks phenomenon illustrates the domino effect of globalization. People once willing to pay $5.00 for a cup of coffee when times were good affect coffee farmers halfway around the world when an economic crisis forces the coffee drinkers to tighten their belts.

The Rwandan farm owner now has sharply reduced buying power. He and his released workers are unable to buy shoes from the Southeast Asian manufacturer. Even their local spending is reduced, resulting in many shopkeepers feeling the pinch. The Italian coffee-machine maker sees a rapid decrease in profits as Starbucks and other companies decide to temporarily stop opening new stores.

How to cope with a crisis is anybody's guess, because most economic crises are the result of many problems. Their effects may be rapid, but the situation itself is often developed over a long period of time. This is why economic analysts talk about the "bubble" when referring to unrealistic economic circumstances. Problems often are widely recognized. But for various reasons, people and countries choose to ignore them. An example with which many of us (whether individuals or countries) can identify is overspending one's financial resources. When expenses can no longer be met, the result is default on loans, which can lead to bankruptcy.

An individual, for example, may use a credit card to buy his or her daily Starbucks latte. Even though the buyer lacks the cash to make the purchase, the idea of paying the bill later is attractive. Day by day, the amount of money owed to credit card companies keeps climbing. In addition to the actual bill, interest continues to build up rapidly. The initial price of a cup of coffee may have been $5.00. Adjusted for interest and various fees, it eventually reaches $8.50 a purchase. Then the credit card issuer decides to change the terms of the coffee drinker's contract (by law it can do that) and increase fees even more. Soon after, the price of a $5.00 latte has ballooned to $11.00. Suddenly, our coffee drinker finds that he or she is in serious financial trouble. Too much money is owed to meet monthly credit card payments.

Poor money management may even be responsible for a person having to declare bankruptcy. When people declare bankruptcy, their debt is not really erased but is spread among other consumers who pay higher fees. Bankruptcy means that an individual will have a hard time receiving loans in the future. If the individual does receive future loans, they will come with a much higher interest rate. No credit lender wants to conduct business with someone who represents a bad investment.

One would expect nations to act smarter than individuals, as they are led by teams of elected and appointed experts. Yet they do not. Nations make mistakes identical to those of individuals.

THE INTERNATIONAL ECONOMIC CRISIS OF 2008

The year 2008 will long be remembered. It brought the worst financial crisis since the Great Depression of the 1930s. In the

United States, years of uncontrolled spending by the federal government, public and private corporations, and individual consumers erupted in crisis. In a matter of weeks, the sinking U.S. economy dragged the rest of the world down with it. Stock markets plummeted, and the supply of money vanished. Large corporations, from banks to newspaper publishers, had to file for bankruptcy protection. They simply did not have money in reserve to continue operating in productive ways.

These companies, just like our coffee drinker, borrowed money from others that they were unable to repay. Many also had made bad investments. With little if any money coming in from their own investments, many companies could not pay back their loans. This condition triggered a financial deadlock on American and international markets. This is what analysts mean when they say that there is no "liquidity" to stimulate recovery.

Why do corporations fall into this kind of trap? The answer is simple. It is much easier to use someone else's money to expand business and make a profit than it is to use one's own. In previous years, when times were good, investment banks would borrow the money from others and invest in, for example, the real-estate business. When the real-estate market was good, prices increased rapidly. The investment, therefore, was growing, and the bankers did not have to do anything except count their money. When they sold, they paid back their original loan and kept the profit for themselves. All this occurred without actually having any of their own money at the beginning. The investment bank was using other people's money—perhaps yours—to make a profit. At the same time, working Americans were offered loans with low interest rates and "zero down payments" in order to purchase homes.

Guess where these attractive offers came from? They came from investment banks that knew if people kept buying houses, their prices would go up. They provided attractive options in a "buy now and pay later" kind of real-estate purchase plan, just to bring more buyers. In fact, millions of Americans who lacked adequate financial resources suddenly were able to buy a home. Sadly, pursuing the "American dream" of home ownership, millions of them fell victim to economic reality. The federal government enthusiastically supported the program of real-estate expansion for people of lower economic status. It did so despite signs of caution warning that doing so was a perilous economic decision. The artificially created real-estate "bubble" eventually had to burst.

CREDIT CARDS

If a person is willing to remain at home and avoid travel anywhere for longer than one day, he or she may get by without credit cards. Today, however, in order to stay in a hotel, rent a vehicle, book an event ticket, or purchase many other products, we cannot avoid using credit cards. Many businesses require credit card deposits instead of cash.

Since they were introduced, credit cards have grown into an industry of unimaginable proportions. At the same time, they have created a situation in which irresponsible use can cause soaring personal debt. Before "plastic," an individual with little cash had few options. If funds were available, money could be spent from a checking account (where checks were accepted). Money could be borrowed from friends or perhaps from a bank. Many stores offered layaway programs or payment plans. Most people simply lived within their means. They did not buy things that they could not afford. With credit cards, however, things changed. The door was opened to seemingly unlimited credit which, in turn, artificially contributed to an increase in one's living standard. The problem was that credit cards never were designed for such a thing. Their purpose was to substitute for already available cash. "Buy now and pay later" eventually became "buy now and then later try to pay a portion of the bill." Every bill unpaid in its entirety carries interest that continues to build the actual debt.

With increased global development, the credit card industry acted accordingly and connected the world in its own way. Visa, MasterCard,

In response to the real-estate crisis, the federal government began to supply money to banks in order to stimulate circulation and investments. But the government also was teetering at the edge of bankruptcy. In order to stimulate the economy, it literally had to create money from nothing. So money was printed and disbursed to the market in the form of loans. To accomplish this, the government had to go into debt just like anyone else. In

and American Express, in particular, serve consumers in almost all countries. International travelers can use their cards without the need to carry a variety of different currencies. Cardholders are rewarded for each purchase by receiving frequent flier miles or points used for some other purpose.

Credit card companies have received a bad reputation, often for rightful reasons. Yet the growth of consumer debt always shows similar trends once individuals acquire the cards. In order to keep up with society, they live beyond their means. In the emerging economies of developing countries, credit cards allow their holders to purchase previously unattainable goods. This and other factors account for the vast amount of debt accumulated prior to the 2008 global financial crisis and credit crunch. Everyone was borrowing while extending their debt burden. In times of crises, credit card agencies suffer as well. This, in turn, causes them to increase fees and further burden consumers.

Regardless of potential difficulties associated with a credit card, this type of transaction is the future of financial interactions in a consumer-focused world. More credit cards already are linked to checking accounts and are known as check (or debit) cards. In such cases, the plastic transaction is connected to the amount of money available in one's account. But the days of spending beyond our means will perhaps never end.

"For Sale" signs litter U.S. neighborhoods (*above*), a result of the economic crisis of 2008. Millions of people who in the past did not qualify for home loans took advantage of the "too good to be true" offers made by banks. After years of expanding, the housing bubble finally burst.

a period of several months during the fall of 2008, the government increased the nation's debt by more than two trillion dollars. This debt imposes a tremendous burden on the country's economic well-being. And it is an obligation that will have to be repaid by future generations of Americans.

The Roots of the Problem

The real-estate market is part of a much larger problem. All aspects of the nation's economy face a shaky reality and a cloudy future. Because they affected so many Americans, problems in the housing market simply have received the most attention. To fully understand just how big the problem is, let's turn the calendar back many decades.

For much of U.S. history, gold was used to back the currency. Printed money could not exceed the value of gold reserves stored at Fort Knox, Kentucky. Therefore, it was not possible to spend money that could not be backed up with an equal amount of gold. The country had to live within its means. What this policy also did was to back the dollar with an existing commodity of comparable value. Gold is the world's most desirable commodity, and that gave a high value to the dollar. As there is only so much gold available, however, the policy did not allow the creation of money that gold reserves cannot back.

The "gold standard" policy created many restrictions that were unpopular with a number of presidential administrations. Between 1913, when the Federal Reserve Banking System was created, and 1971, the United States completely removed the gold standard. President Richard Nixon's administration dealt the final blow to the dollar-backed-with-gold reserves. What did the government decide to use as an alternative to gold? Nothing! Since 1971, American currency has not been backed with anything except a nice promise that debts are going to be repaid. This means that the government can print as much currency as it wishes as long as someone will buy it (meaning other countries such as China, Saudi Arabia, or Japan). Then it can use the money to fund wars, construction projects, social welfare programs, or anything else.

Not surprisingly, the national debt has skyrocketed since the 1970s. Without restrictions, the line of credit was unlimited. Free of limits, the federal government simply kept spending more than it made through taxes. Banking system regulations also were relaxed. Instead of being able to back all of their investments, the banks had to have only 10 percent of their actual funds invested. What does this mean? It means that your bank could use 90 percent of the money from *your* account to conduct business elsewhere. The bank needed to back its investment with only 10 cents on the dollar. With this arrangement, banks kept giving loans to investments that ultimately proved to be unsound. Is it any wonder that the entire system eventually collapsed?

Let's illustrate the foregoing at a less abstract level. If someone wants to borrow money from you, you have two options. The first is to sign an agreement that the individual can borrow money in the amount of land he owns. Your loan is now secured. If he fails to pay it back to you, his land will belong to you. You can sell the land and return your investment. The second is for the person to tell you that if you lend him the money, he will pay you back later after he gets some money. How? Well, no one really knows for sure. Which option would you choose? What if you were the one who needed a loan?

The result of fiscal policy in which the value of the dollar is not backed by anything has resulted in a decline in the value of American currency. During the twentieth century, the dollar lost more than 90 percent of its value. While this happened, the national debt increased to unimaginable levels. In early 2009, it amounted to nearly $11 trillion, a sum that is close to the country's annual gross domestic product (GDP)!

Spilling Over

As the U.S. economy is the world's largest by a wide margin, what affects the United States soon reaches across the globe. Much of the latest global crisis began with economic problems in this country. But the United States is not alone in this regard. A closer look at many other national economies reveals they, too, have made similar mistakes. And problems are not limited to poor, developing countries in Africa or Asia. They can strike anywhere. Tiny Iceland, economically and politically one of the world's most stable countries, became a victim of economic adventurism.

An island in the northern Atlantic, Iceland is physically quite remote from global financial markets. As global connections illustrate, physical remoteness means nothing anymore. Now everyone can act as a player in order to gain a share of the profits. Icelanders thought so too. After all, they became recognized as a reasonable, well-educated, and realistic people. Icelanders transformed their rugged volcanic island into one of the world's wealthiest nations on a per capita basis. With only 320,000 people, Iceland is a small country. Economic decisions are carefully scrutinized before plans are implemented.

MAKING C⊕NNECTI⊕NS

Despite the erosion of currency value because of inflation, many still believe that the best way to become wealthy is to save money. A good portion of today's millionaires began to save and invest their earnings at a young age. Throughout the years, interest grew and they kept reinvesting. Even with periodic market slowdowns and financial crises, sound investments pay off.

Companies also pay dividends on investment in their stocks. If a person invested $1,000 in Philip Morris stock in 1980, then reinvested dividends, that money would have reached $250,000 some 20 years later. All one has to do is be patient. Yet, patience is not something that many people, particularly the young, possess. Long-term investments that pay off decades in the future are no longer attractive to most people. This trend is not only noticeable among contemporary Americans. The worldwide impact of popular culture, where *now* and *fast* are hallmark terms, is affecting other cultures.

After all, who is to blame when success stories portrayed in the media are usually about people who became wealthy overnight? On the other hand, it is the short-term risk-taking that creates such success stories. Which option do you believe would be the most appropriate, not only for you but also for young people in other countries? Would you be better off slowly compounding interest over time or throwing everything into one risk-taking option?

In an attempt to profit from the global economic boom of recent years, Iceland's banks invested heavily in international markets. For example, they offered savings accounts with higher interest rates than in Western Europe. This strategy attracted many new customers from the European mainland. The banks, in turn, invested the money. This way they could make a handsome profit even after paying the higher interest to their customers. The system worked well until the global downturn erased the value of investments. Ultimately, the banks lost huge amounts of money. They were unable to pay interest on existing savings accounts and, in fact, people were unable to withdraw their savings. Under the strain, Iceland's entire financial system collapsed.

It is estimated that Iceland's banks and other institutions created a debt 10 times greater than the country's gross national product. Iceland's economy generates about $10 billion per year. Yet it finds itself owing an incredible $100 billion to various creditors. The country is bankrupt. Its currency crumbled, and the government canceled trading. People stood in disbelief when they suddenly realized that their life savings were gone. The government has limited options, one of which is to beg for loans from other countries already leery of Iceland's ability to pay them back.

CONSEQUENCES

Depending on their intensity, economic crises can create dire political and social consequences. Survival is a natural human characteristic, and when times get worse, people act accordingly. Lack of financial strength often leaves political leaders with little choice but to implement unpopular measures. For example, they can increase taxes, reduce salaries, or cut back on welfare programs. In the business world, unemployment rises as corporations try to minimize financial losses by reducing their workforce. This imposes an additional burden on agencies that provide unemployment compensation. Eventually, a complex cycle of frustration is created with few positive short-term options.

During such difficult times, civil unrest can explode in violence. People take to the streets and demand changes. In Greece during the fall of 2008, growing public dissatisfaction erupted in a violent rampage that spread to cities throughout the country. The incident that sparked the riots was unrelated to economic and political issues. Nonetheless, the demonstrators immediately turned their anger against the government and its economic policies. Greece, too, suffered from the global economic downturn. Soon after, similar types of incidents spread across Europe, led by people inspired by the Greek rumble.

Today, most developed countries are able to rebound quite rapidly from economic misfortune. Their economies are diversified; that is, in an economic sense their eggs are not all in one basket, so to speak. They are able to adjust to difficult circumstances and gradually work their way out of a crisis. Developing countries face a much steeper slope on their path to economic recovery. Their economies have a weak service sector and usually depend upon one or two basic sources of revenue. It is not uncommon for a sharp drop to occur in the demand for or price of various commodities. If this happens to the item(s) upon which a country's economy depends, the entire country may fall into disarray. A falling economy and weak government open the door for civil unrest, escalating conflict, and even civil war. Numerous examples across the globe show that economic prosperity is essential to a peaceful coexistence. Economic hardship almost always leads to conflict.

COOPERATION
AND PROTECTION

A s you now realize, it is practically impossible for a country (or person!) to function outside the global economic system. Some nations limit their exposure to ongoing economic trends. Others wholeheartedly embrace cooperative involvement. Regardless of varying individual degrees of interaction, a certain amount of involvement is required.

Switzerland chose not to join the European Union (EU). The small mountainous country is landlocked in the heart of Europe and entirely surrounded by EU members. Yet the Swiss firmly believe that their destiny lies in their own hands. Unlike neighboring countries that adopted the euro, Switzerland remains faithful to its own currency. The Swiss are known for protecting their own sovereignty. They believe that membership in organizations such as the European Union would limit their national freedoms. As one of the world's wealthiest nations, Switzerland has an approach to economic survival that has been successful.

The countries of Eastern Europe, on the other hand, willingly put aside issues of national independence in order to cooperate economically. Many of them became members of the EU. They had few options. Following the economic neglect of the Communist era, they desperately needed to promote economic development.

WORLD TRADE ORGANIZATION

Following World War II, there was a desperate need to rebuild war-ravaged countries. Previous attempts to create a cooperative world organization met with little success. Many people, however, realized that there was an urgent need for such a system. Out of this idea, the United Nations (UN) was born. In 1945, the year the war ended, the UN replaced the defunct League of Nations. In 1939, the league failed to prevent the eruption of global conflict that led to the Second World War. In 1947, UN leaders agreed on the formation of an economic body with the purpose of regulating international economic relations. The new organization was named the General Agreement on Tariffs and Trade (GATT). In 1995, GATT became the World Trade Organization (WTO).

The main purpose of the WTO is to help resolve trade disagreements that arise between member countries. Membership is voluntary but requires the approval of existing members. In some cases, members may have an issue with an applicant country. When this occurs, the approval process may drag on for years until both sides are satisfied. Russia, for example, applied for membership in 1993 but is still waiting to be accepted as a member. Issues range from inability to protect intellectual property created elsewhere (software piracy) to policies on energy and agriculture subsidies.

The WTO steps in to mediate conflicts when members cannot reach agreements in bilateral trade relationships. This often occurs between the United States and the European Union, the two largest economies. As they are involved in extremely complex interactions, not everything operates smoothly every time. Other countries that may have a stake in the issue choose sides based upon which outcome is in their own self-interests.

The Banana War

The so-called Banana War is a good example of an issue that separates American and European economic interests. The conflict began in the early 1990s when the EU introduced higher tariffs for bananas imported from Latin American countries. At the same time, the tariffs were lowered for bananas imported from African countries (mainly former British and French colonies). A Latin American banana producer, for example, might pay $150 more per metric ton of bananas than an African competitor. In a business that involves millions of tons of bananas each year, the figure represents a considerable loss in revenue for Latin American producers. Europe, with a half-billion consumers, represents a market that producers cannot avoid. Latin American banana producers simply asked for fair treatment.

If the Banana War is between Latin America and Europe, what role does the United States play in the conflict? Shouldn't we simply mind our own business and leave others to theirs? But the answer is not that simple. U.S. corporations have invested billions of dollars in developing banana plantations throughout much of tropical Latin America. And these companies harvest immense profits from international trade. Any attempt to limit market access to Latin American bananas is a strike against the U.S. economy.

As Europe continued with tariffs on bananas, America retaliated by imposing some of its own. The Clinton administration implemented tariffs on a variety of luxury goods imported from the European Union. Who paid the price? Consumers, of course, each time they shopped in a grocery or department store. French perfumes and gourmet cheeses increased in price to adjust to

A seemingly simple act of selling bananas to non-tropical areas turned into an economic battle involving the United States and Britain. *Above,* a worker sorts bananas at a fruit and vegetable market in Panama City.

new tariffs. So did German and Belgian chocolates. The two sides tried to find an agreement but failed. As of early 2009, discussions mediated by the WTO continue to search for a solution to the banana conflict that both sides can accept. By now, however, other countries in Latin America and Africa have joined the talks, thereby further clouding the issue. Little did you know that your breakfast banana played a significant role in a heated international controversy!

Preferential Treatment or Loss of Sovereignty?

The structure of the WTO allows each country only one vote in its decision-making process. This system reduces the impact of powerful nations over small and seemingly insignificant countries. WTO supporters agree that everyone should have an equal voice in matters that relate to the complex global economic system. Not everyone shares this opinion. Some still believe that large and powerful countries receive preferential treatment. They question why anyone should care about some small African country that mostly produces bananas. Rather, members tend to side with countries with which they already have a strong partnership or may benefit from in the future. Others see the WTO as an extended arm of political decision making by leading powers.

Some present WTO members are dissatisfied. They resent the loss of independence when the organization's decisions

REACHING BEYOND LAND TO SEA AND SPACE

Successful development of global connections must include cooperation between countries for goods to flow from producers to consumers. In Europe, for example, Russian oil and natural gas must be transported from Siberian fields through a network of pipelines. Germany is the largest consumer of Russian energy. During the Soviet era, only one country, Poland, stood between producer and consumer. Today, Russia must follow agreements with transit countries, such as Belarus and Ukraine, just to reach Poland. A hefty royalty is paid to all countries through which pipelines pass. Obviously, Russia wants an uninterrupted flow of gas and oil to Germany. Russia also tries to reach the market by more direct routes. Recently it worked closely with Germans (in the Baltic Sea) and Turks (in the Black Sea) to create deep-sea pipelines.

Seas and oceans are only seemingly quiet. Deep beneath their blue surface lies a dense network of fiber-optic cables that connect much of the globe. These cables transport a huge amount of information in a heartbeat of time. The cables carry telephone calls and other don't go their way. This is of particular importance to powerful countries such as the United States. Many politicians voice strong opposition to American participation in the WTO and similar organizations. They believe that membership undermines traditional values of a free market. And they resent that other countries can impose regulatory measures that limit U.S. economic activities in the international marketplace. Critics argue that American voters did not directly approve joining the WTO through the electoral process. Moreover, America must follow measures designed by an international body, instead of the U.S. Congress. When possible, it is best to have global connections with other nations decided upon by direct negotiations between the countries involved.

telecommunication exchanges. They also transport Internet-related data, from stock market information to duels between video game junkies. Such a network is expensive and difficult to build and maintain, but the benefits are tremendous. Global cooperation is necessary because information must flow between countries without interruption.

During the mid-twentieth century and the heat of the Cold War, space became a geographically strategic location. The Soviets launched the first satellite in 1957, and the Americans followed soon after. Both sides eventually realized the need to open the skies to commercial use. In the 1970s, a direct satellite link provided the first transmission of a live sporting event across the world. Today, many nations utilize this opportunity for a wide variety of economic purposes. They send satellites to orbit Earth and monitor environmental changes. Multinational cooperation has contributed to the creation of a large station for scientific research (and space tourism). Most recently, private enterprises received approval for their own space exploration.

FREE TRADE

To bolster trade and generate a better overall relationship, countries occasionally create free trade agreements. Removal of trade barriers, customs, and tariffs involves prior negotiation between two or more governments. The goal is to create conditions in which goods flow without interruptions and with market-determined prices. Access to markets is open to everyone. Such relationships increase competitiveness between corporations. This, in turn, ultimately benefits consumers in all countries. Under this arrangement, consumer options increase greatly in terms of the variety and price of products.

Corporations, too, benefit from free trade agreements. They can find the most ideal location for an assembly plant or service center. Its location need not be within the country itself. An American company, for example, might initially be located in some foreign country, let's say Argentina. Ecuador, however, can offer much less expensive land, energy, and labor costs. The company is free to move its plant to take advantage of the economic opportunities in Ecuador. Production costs will decrease, thereby lowering the product's cost to American shoppers.

As the global economic system becomes more intertwined, free trade may blossom. This should be a natural progression of trends because many multinational corporations already operate worldwide. One of the most evident economic changes is how adaptive international business operations have become in recent times. With free trade agreements, the flow of capital and labor is uninterrupted, and cutting-edge technologies dictate business trends. In Northern America and Western Europe, the workforce is aging. If the door is open to immigration, retirees can be replaced by foreign workers. This is an arrangement from which everyone benefits. Foreign investments also increase in developing nations engaged in free trade with the developed world. The inflow of foreign capital helps to increase employment and the quality of life in poor countries.

The North American Free Trade Agreement (NAFTA) is perhaps the best-known cooperative economic arrangement. In 1993, representatives from the United States, Canada, and Mexico signed documents removing existing barriers. NAFTA became the world's largest free trade zone. Each country loosened its trade restrictions, and all have benefited in some way from the freer flow of goods. Mexican communities near the American border rapidly expanded their industrial capacity. Workers from central and southern Mexico flocked to find employment there, while American companies took advantage of affordable labor.

Not everyone supports NAFTA, however, and some critics seek revisions of the agreement. American labor unions worry about employment outsourcing and loss of American jobs. Environmental organizations point to widespread air and water pollution and loss of soil fertility due to poor farming practices. There are even those who worry that Canada, the United States, and Mexico will eventually unite. They fear that the day will come when there will be a single country with a common government and currency. The perception that the U.S. economy is not well protected is a frequently discussed topic in state and federal legislatures. To prevent further decline of America's autonomy, some politicians call for protective measures and greater economic isolation.

PROTECTIONISM

Calls for removal of economic barriers often fail because interests do not align. A country may see a need to protect sectors of its economy that are struggling. Or it may have problems with certain national security issues if its borders become more open. Sometimes barriers are erected only by the "politics as usual" principle. As the Banana War example illustrated, most countries rely on some type of protectionist policies. They are designed to benefit domestic businesses at the expense of imported goods.

In the United States, the agricultural sector of the economy receives large subsidies from the federal government. To grow certain crops, farmers are rewarded financially. For example, as Americans searched for alternative fuels, Midwestern farmers responded. They increased the production of corn to support a growing ethanol industry. But ethanol produced from corn falls far short of being profitable. Production expenses are high compared to the energy produced. Ethanol from sugar cane is a much better option. But cane cannot be grown on the northern plains because of the short growing season. The Corn Belt states from Indiana to North Dakota also are important to politicians, both Republican and Democrat. Local politicians are aware that chances for reelection are slim if one chooses not to support ethanol production. Therefore, they continue to support large agricultural subsidies, whether for corn to be used in the manufacture of ethanol or other agricultural commodities. The legislators vote against any bills that may change existing conditions. They also vote for provisions that limit quotas and raise tariffs on imported fuels.

The steel industry was once a major driving force of American development. Eventually, however, it was no longer able to match the quality and price of foreign steel. In a system of free trade, American steel producers would go out of business. But with the government's help, they continue to compete. Added tariffs on imported steel keep domestic steel producers competitive and thousands of workers employed. Electoral battleground states like Pennsylvania, where the steel industry is strong, listen carefully to what presidential candidates say in regard to global trade relationships. Candidates favoring the removal of trade barriers often are reminded to retune their message when visiting Pennsylvania.

Protectionism is an age-old measure. Unfortunately, it will continue in the future, although perhaps with less impact than previously. Although it may have some short-term benefits for a country, in the long run it is counterproductive. Protectionist policies do not allow industries and places to transform on their own. And they restrict a country's ability to find new niches in international business affairs. They are mainly designed to patch up a business model full of continuously expanding holes. A fundamental rule of good business is that if a company cannot compete, it should fail. When a government artificially supports a noncompetitive business, it may survive for some time. When the failure finally occurs, however, it comes with a bang and with a heavy cost to taxpayers and consumers.

MAKING CONNECTIONS

MONEY LAUNDERING AND TAX EVASION

Did you ever wonder why every traveler to the United States must indicate whether he or she is carrying cash in excess of $10,000? The regulation is designed to prevent international money laundering and transport of finances for criminal activities. International drug cartels are experts in smuggling. But once they acquire money, they need it to appear as legitimate income. Terrorist organizations use money laundering operations to fund cells in different countries. Even the rogue forces in some governments create programs to bypass legal channels (for example, the Iran-Contra Affair of the 1980s). In some cases, a country may become involved in a money laundering scheme. That occurs when a nation is under international sanctions and is not allowed to fully participate in the global banking system (for example, Yugoslavia during the 1990s).

Money laundering poses a serious threat to the world economic system. This is why most countries are willing to cooperate in its prevention. Billions of dollars are transferred annually from illegal to legal enterprises. Tax evasion, however, is an even larger problem. Corporations and wealthy individuals take shelter in tax havens—places where taxes are not imposed upon their wealth—around the world. Once they manage to transfer finances to offshore accounts, these finances become difficult to monitor. Such activities can cost a country billions of dollars in lost revenue.

DIALOGUE

The Group of Eight, or G8, provides an example of today's changing economic world. Each year, leaders of the world's eight most developed countries meet to discuss pressing political and economic issues. The summit includes presidents and prime ministers from the United States, Canada, Western Europe, and Japan. In recent years Russia, too, became a member of this exclusive group. Other countries may eventually be invited to join. China, India, and Brazil are among the world's fastest growing economies. In fact, they soon may overtake some of the original G8 members in economic strength and gross national product. Positive global changes have contributed to the expansion of wealth in previously unimaginable places. During the 1970s and 1980s, Brazil was known for its political struggles, vast debt, and wildly out of control hyperinflation. The country is now a model of successful economic and political progress.

China, India, and Brazil combine to account for nearly three billion of the world's people. As their economic power grows, other countries sense the need for dialogue with these economically emerging nations. Annual G8 meetings are designed for the leaders to spend time in a relaxed setting with one another. The environment tends to be informal, and leaders are not expected to follow strict diplomatic protocols. Here discussion occurs in a more private setting and is conducted without public interference. Economic issues are always the top priority.

FUTURE GLOBAL ECONOMY

In times when economic difficulties are on everyone's mind, questions about the future are unavoidable. The cyclical nature of the global economic system reminds us that after each hardship a time of renewal arrives. Stock markets rebound, production of goods increases, and trade interaction strengthens. Then after some period of time another downturn occurs, and once again people have to tighten their belts. No one can exactly predict the full scope of economic development. If someone could, he or she would become the world's wealthiest person! What can be predicted is that global economic connections will increase in the future. And they will be highly beneficial to the entire global community.

THE ROLE OF TECHNOLOGY
Technology certainly will play a significant role in future economic changes. Historically, technological accomplishments

have been the keys to economic growth and development. The Industrial Revolution, for example, was the primary key to the economic development that has occurred during the past two centuries. It is difficult to imagine the world today had the steam engine not been developed. The same holds true for electricity, the automobile, the computer, and many other technological developments that have boosted the global economy in the past.

Human attempts to create technological improvements rank as perhaps the most important economic driving force. The Agricultural Revolution occurred because humans were curious about how certain plants could be put to practical use. Yet the

ELECTRONIC MEDIA

Not too many people remember times when the "rabbit ears" TV antenna represented an advanced technological feature. Without it, however, many Americans never would have experienced the Super Bowl at home or Neil Armstrong's walk on the moon. For decades, viewers relied on Walter Cronkite, the "most trusted man in America," to deliver the evening news. Only three major television networks existed: CBS, NBC, and ABC. Program options were few, and watchers got used to it. After all, it was still more exciting than radio—except, of course, when Orson Welles unintentionally created panic with his production of H.G. Wells's *War of the Worlds*. The twentieth-century technological revolution changed our views, but also our economic behavior as consumers.

The economic potential of electronic media always has been thought to be endless. In the 1980s, a giant leap forward occurred with the spread of cable television. Hundreds of channels now covered everything from music to continuous news coverage. Satellite transmission allowed us to eyewitness major events without delay. In the 1990s, the Internet entered our lives. Today we cannot function revolution did not stop with wheat or barley. It continues today. After the first grain was planted, early farmers immediately wondered how to improve yields. Several millennia later, scientists still work on the development of new species. This is why we can grow certain plants in previously unimaginable environments. A ride through Arizona or California is enough to help us understand that deserts are not wastelands. They can be transformed into very productive agricultural areas. Today, rice is the world's primary foodstuff. The nutritious grain has evolved to more than 20,000 different varieties as the result of scientific modification. Without continuously evolving technological capabilities, such improvements would not have been possible.

without its features, from e-mail to video exchanges to social networking Web sites. Television stations have gradually shifted their attention to the Internet. Printed media, too, has realized the need to adapt to the needs of a new generation. Articles are delivered through cell phones, while online videos and slide shows are now commonplace. Stores renting or selling movies are losing customers to online services. Why drive to pick up a DVD when it can be downloaded off the Internet?

What the future of electronic media will bring is hard to imagine because new ideas are introduced seemingly every week. One thing, however, is sure. The world of electronic media is an enormous business that revolves around economic trends. Advertisements and other aspects of marketing have reached the farthest corners of the Internet. Online shopping alone generates profits measured in the billions of dollars. Spam messages attempting to sell something, from vitamins to fake insurance policies, flood in-boxes. Although the Internet was not invented for such purposes, the economic reasons have become the driving force of change, even in the virtual world.

Imagine improvements in communication technology. In the old days, people communicated through messengers riding their horses across the country, just to deliver a single message. Sometimes they used pigeons. Then came railroads and the telegraph. How about today? Each time another technological breakthrough has occurred, it has benefited economic interaction. Global positioning systems (GPS) were initially developed for military purposes. Early on it was recognized that GPS can be beneficial for civilian purposes and can bring a variety of improvements. Shipping lanes on the high seas are controlled through such navigation. Even planting and harvesting crops in the American Midwest is conducted with the help of GPS. Computers control the exact amount of seeds needed for planting and harvesting record yields. This information is communicated to tractors or combines (harvesting machines) in the field, telling them how to operate.

New technology lowers expenses, which in turn lowers the price of products. Transportation expenses decreased significantly when refrigerated trucks were invented. This allowed shipment of frozen products without fear of losing merchandise. A look at grocery shelves reveals the rich diversity of products offered to consumers. We have more to choose from than ever before.

Exploration for new energy resources will certainly receive a boost from advancements in technology. As much as fossil fuels served as the backbone of the global economy in the twentieth century, a new type of energy will act similarly in the twenty-first century. What exactly will replace the much maligned fossil fuels is difficult to predict. Perhaps we may return to nuclear energy with renewed enthusiasm.

The most radical contribution from technological development will be advancements in information exchange. In a traditional work environment, a certain physical arrangement was understood for a proper corporate setting. Managers would gather around the table and brainstorm new plans and policies. Workers spent their time in assembly areas, but in the same factory as

Developing technology has a tremendous impact on the global economy. Improvements to agriculture practices, including the use of GPS systems (*above*) lead to larger and better crops.

the management. In the future, such arrangements will be found only in references to relic business practices.

Ownership and management do not have to be in close proximity with production facilities. Owners increasingly have little oversight of actual production and distribution. That duty is assigned to lower-level management. New ideas about how to run businesses are created elsewhere. In the latest international business environment, "elsewhere" means not just across the country, but across the globe. The ability to exchange information has created the need for a rapid transformation of business practices. In order to succeed, companies not only must have an excellent product but also must show agility in following global trends. The reaction time has drastically shortened during the last decade. What used to be measured in months and years is now measured in hours and days. A company in the past had enough time to make adjustments (for example, introduce a new line of cars prior to ending an existing line), but today's market demands immediate reaction. Otherwise a company will not be able to sell its product to consumers. Future demands will be even more rigorous because everything in the world is changing so rapidly.

INTEGRATION

The result of changes will undoubtedly be further global economic integration. International cooperation, under the influence of economic forces, will contribute to the distribution of wealth into less developed countries. This does not mean that everyone will become equally wealthy. After all, the purpose of economic interaction is that one party generates profit from another. The rich will remain rich. The poor, on the other hand, will have a much better chance to exit poverty. Compared to past trends, global conditions will improve. The increase in quality of life will affect even the most remote and politically isolated places.

Migration from poorer to richer areas of the world will increase. There is no reason for anyone to feel that his or her own country is the only place to look for a better future. The need for more laborers has reached alarming levels in many developed nations. Developing countries, too, will begin to feel the pressure of the need to replenish their workforces.

Economic development is going to create awesome social changes. It is difficult to determine whether such changes will be good or bad. One thing is certain—personal wealth generates the need for individual liberties. How this will affect countries like China, with a booming economy and an oppressive government, is difficult to predict. Even before the Communists gained control, the Chinese lived in a strong hierarchical society. The masses have followed orders from their leaders for centuries.

All decisions were created with disregard for the needs of individuals. Now when so many Chinese can decide about their own prosperity, the questions of liberty are being voiced more and more frequently.

The same holds true for India. There, for example, traditional barriers of caste and social separation are slowly fading away. Divorce rates among the educated and those living abroad are on the increase. For thousands of years, marriages were arranged and females had very little individual freedom. As Indian women no longer have to rely on family members, they can choose their own destiny. Today, many women chart their own route to the future, rather than follow a path set by others into a social blind alley. Other parts of the world will experience similar changes which, once they are underway, are unstoppable. The idea of freedom is one of the most powerful forces in the world!

Regardless of how the future unfolds, the economy will be the primary driving force of change. As historical evidence suggests and geographic reality additionally supports, globalization will continue in only one direction: forward.

GLOSSARY

alternative fuels   Fuels that, unlike fossil fuels, are not in conventional use and are renewable.

capitalism   An economic system based on private ownership of capital.

Federal Reserve   The central bank of the United States, created in 1913. Its system covers 12 regional reserve banks.

GATT   General Agreement on Tariffs and Trade; an agency created in 1948, predecessor to the World Trade Organization.

globalization   Growth and integration on a global scale; usage differs slightly on the basis of context.

Great Depression   Period of rapid economic decline that began in the aftermath of the Stock Market crash of 1929; it lasted through the 1930s in the United States and affected the rest of the world.

inflation   Increase in prices of consumer goods and services that leads to decline in purchasing power for consumers. Monetary inflation is the increase in the government's supply of notes into markets, which also decreases value of currency and purchasing power for consumers.

NAFTA   North American Free Trade Agreement, between the United States, Canada, and Mexico, created in 1993. Its purpose is to stimulate removal of trade barriers and increase economic interaction among the countries.

oil sands   The world's largest deposits of petroleum and a potentially vast resource for fossil fuel exploration besides traditional drilling methods; majority of such deposits are in Canada and Venezuela.

socialism   An economic system in which ownership of the means of production, distribution, and exchange of wealth is made and maintained by community and state rather than by private individuals or corporations.

WTO   World Trade Organization; an international body that succeeded GATT in 1995. It serves the purpose of mediation in international economic affairs between member countries.

 # BIBLIOGRAPHY

Griffiths, Robert, ed. *Annual Editions: Developing World 08/09.* Dubuque, IA: McGraw-Hill, 2007.

Schultz, Theodore W. *Investing in People: The Economics of Population Quality.* Berkeley, CA: University of California Press, 1981.

Simon, Julian L. *The Ultimate Resource 2.* Princeton, NJ: Princeton University Press, 1996.

Smith, Adam. *The Wealth of Nations.* New York, NY: Random House (Bantam Classics), 2003.

U.S. Department of Energy, Energy Information Adminstration. http://www.eia.doe.gov/

U.S. National Debt Clock. http://brillig.com/debt_clock/

World Trade Organization. http://www.wto.org/

FURTHER RESOURCES

Epping, Randy Charles. *A Beginner's Guide to the World Economy.* New York, NY: Vintage Books, 1992.

Friedman, Thomas L. *The World Is Flat 3.0: A Brief History of the Twenty-First Century.* New York, NY: Picador, 2007.

Geisst, Charles R. *Encyclopedia of American Business History,* 2 Volumes. New York, NY: Facts On File, 2005.

Wiggin, Addison, and Kate Incontrera. *I.O.U.S.A.: One Nation. Under Stress. In Debt.* Hoboken, NJ: John Wiley & Sons, 2008.

PICTURE CREDITS

Page

14: Zhong fan zh / AP Images

22: Jerome Delay / AP Images

27: © Ashraf Amra / APA / Landov

37: David Longstreath / AP Images

43: Lauren Victoria Burke / AP Images

51: Sun hai / AP Images

57: Rodrique Ngowi/ AP Images

64: Liu jian xj / AP Images

69: Ken Salazar / AP Images

75: Bebeto Matthews / AP Images

80: Nick Ut / AP Images

89: Kathryn Cook/ AP Images

101: Seth Perlman / AP Images

INDEX

ABOUT THE AUTHOR

ZORAN PAVLOVIĆ is a professional geographer and regular contributor to several Chelsea House Publishing series. His books include *Europe* for MODERN WORLD CULTURES and more than a half-dozen titles for the MODERN WORLD NATIONS series.

 # ABOUT THE EDITOR

CHARLES F. GRITZNER is Distinguished Professor of Geography at South Dakota State University in Brookings. He began college teaching and conducting geographic research in 1960. In addition to teaching, he enjoys travel, writing, working with teachers, and sharing his love for geography with readers. As a senior consulting editor and frequent author for Chelsea House Publishers' MODERN WORLD NATIONS, MAJOR WORLD CULTURES, EXTREME ENVIRONMENTS, and GLOBAL CONNECTIONS series, he has a wonderful opportunity to combine each of these "hobbies." Dr. Gritzner has served as both president and executive director of the National Council for Geographic Education and has received the council's highest honor, the George J. Miller Award for Distinguished Service to Geographic Education, as well as other honors from the NCGE, Association of American Geographers, and other organizations.